MW01179201

Forts

&

Fields

Michigan's Military Places
1669-2014

Dan Heaton

Branden Books, Boston

© Copyright 2014
Branden Books

Library of Congress Cataloging-in-Publication Data

Heaton, Daniel J.
  Forts & fields : Michigan's military places, 1669-2014 / Dan Heaton.
      pages cm
  Includes bibliographical references and index.
  ISBN 978-0-8283-2515-8 (pbk. : alk. paper) 1. Michigan--History, Military. 2. Fortification--Michigan--History. 3. Military bases--Michigan--History. I. Title.
  F566.H38 2014
  355.009774--dc23

                                        2014009158

ISBN 9780828325158 Paperback
ISBN 9780828325165 E-Book

Branden Books
PO Box 812094
Wellesley MA 02482
www.brandenbooks.com

Introduction

Though it is a border state, Michigan is probably not the state that first pops to mind when the average American thinks about his country's military accomplishments. George Washington and his Continental Army never stepped foot in the state. Though it was a part of the Union at the time, Michigan is hundreds of miles away from the nearest Civil War battlefield. Though it has more coastline than another other of the 48 continental states, Michigan has no major naval base from which to launch a mighty fleet.

If one looks a bit deeper into Michigan's history and geography, however, one quickly discovers that the state has a wealth of military history. It is indeed a border state and was the source of a number of key battles in the early portion of the War of 1812. Like other states, Michigan mustered thousands of men to serve in the War Between the States, once even prompting President Abraham Lincoln to utter, "Thank God for Michigan!" During World War II, the state's largest city – Detroit -- became the nation's Arsenal of Democracy. During the Cold War, a series of missile batteries and several air bases were established to protect Detroit's industrial might.

From the days of Sieur De La Salle and Father Jacques Marquette through to the modern age, it has always been more than just dots on the map that have been part of Michigan's military story. Michigan's military story took shape at Civil War mustering-in camps that existed for only a few weeks in the early days of that bitter war and at modern-day Coast Guard stations charged with the preservation life for those who sail the Great Lakes. Before them came forts built by French explorers seeking to corner the fur trade. Later, it was British soldiers expanding their mighty empire and then Americans preparing pilots for two world wars.

These are the stories of Michigan's forts and fields, the military places where men and women served, fought and sometimes died during the march of history.

Contents

Locations by County

Alger
Grand Marias Air Force Station

Alpena
Alpena Combat Readiness Training Center

Benzie
Station Frankfort

Berrien
Fort St. Joseph

Calhoun
Camp Smith
Custer Air Force Station
Fort Custer

Charlevoix
Station Charlevoix

Chippewa
Fort Brady
Fort Drummond
Fort Repentigny
Kincheloe Air Force Base
Raco Army Air Field
Sault Ste. Marie Air Force Station
Sector Sault Ste. Marie

Crawford
Camp Grayling

Grand Traverse
Air Station Traverse City

Houghton
Calumet Air Force Station
Station Portage

Huron
Port Austin Air Force Station
Station Harbor Beach

Iosco
Station Tawas
Wurtsmith Air Force Base

Jackson
Camp Blair

Keweenaw
Fort Wilkins

Leelanau
Empire Air Force Station

Lenawee
Camp Williams

Livingston
Camp Eaton

Mackinac
Fort de Buade
Fort Holmes
Fort Ignatius
Fort Mackinac
Fort Michilimackinac
Station St. Ignace

Macomb
Air Station Detroit
Camp Butler
Selfridge Air National Guard Base
Camp Stockton
Detroit Arsenal (Tank Plant/TACOM)
Station St. Clair Shores

Manistee
Station Manistee

Marquette
Big Bay Firing Range
ELF Tower
KI Sawyer Air Force Base
Station Marquette

Mason
Station Ludington

Monroe
River Raisin National Battlefield Park
Wayne Stockade

Muskegon
Station Muskegon
U.S.S. Silversides

Oakland
Polar Bear Monument

Ottawa
Sector Field Office Grand Haven
Station Holland

Saginaw
Fort Saginaw
Tri-City Army Air Field

St. Clair
Fort Gratiot
Fort St. Joseph
Fort Sinclair
Station Port Huron

St. Joseph
Camp Hogan
Fort Miami
Station St. Joseph

Washtenaw
Willow Run Air Force Station

Wayne
Brodhead Armory
Camp Backus
Camp Banks
Camp Lyon
Camp Ward
Detroit Arsenal (Dearborn)
Detroit Barracks
Detroit Light Guard Armory
Fort Lernoult/Fort Shelby/Fort Detroit
Fort Pontchartrain
Fort Wayne
Grosse Ile Stockade
Naval Air Station Grosse Ile
Romulus Army Air Field
Sector Detroit
Station Belle Isle

Chapter 1

An MH-65 Dolphin rescue helicopter from Coast Guard Air Station Detroit flies past downtown Detroit along the Detroit River. Air crews from the station provide search and rescue services for the entire eastern half of the Great Lakes. (U.S. Coast Guard)

Name: Air Station Detroit
Location: Harrison Township. (Macomb County) (on Selfridge Air National Guard Base)
Established: June 1966
Disposition: Still in operation
Owners: U.S.
Interesting fact: Provides air rescue services along more than 1,100 miles of shoreline
Web site: http://www.uscg.mil/d9/airstaDetroit/default.asp

For several generations, orange rescue helicopters flown by the U.S. Coast Guard have been responded to the distress calls of mariners and pleasure boat operators on the Great Lakes. The Coast Guard's Air Station Detroit, one of two such facilities on the Great Lakes, has never actually had its own, private address. Air Station Detroit was commissioned in June 1966, with an original compliment of 10 officers and 29 enlisted personnel, along with three HH-52A Seaguard helicopters. Since that time, the Air Station has provided 24-hour search and rescue and other services to the Great Lakes region. For about the first three years of its existence, Air Station Detroit was located at NAS Grosse Ile (see page 144). When that facility closed in 1969, the Air Station was relocated to Selfridge Air National Guard Base (see page 168) and it has operated there ever since.

Today, the Air Station operates with just over 100 personnel and conducts more than 300 search and rescue operations every year. Its five assigned MH-65 Dolphin helicopters log about 3,200 flying hours in a typical year.

In addition to operations at Selfridge, Air Station Detroit provides the helicopter, manpower and oversight of Air Facility Muskegon (see page 183), which operates during the heavy boating season, Memorial Day to Labor Day.

Chapter 2

An MH-65 Dolphin rescue helicopter from Coast Guard Air Station Traverse City prepares to land at the station, which is co-located with the Cherry Capital Airport in Traverse City. The station serves the western half of the Great Lakes system.

Name: Air Station Traverse City
Location: Traverse City (Grand Traverse County)
Established: 1946
Disposition: Still in operation
Owners: U.S.
Interesting fact: The older of the two Coast Guard air stations in Michigan
Web site: http://www.uscg.mil/d9/airstatraversecity-/default.asp

Created shortly after World War II and originally assigned a single PBY-5A Catalina fixed-wing float plane, Air Station Traverse City is located adjacent to, and shares a runway with, Cherry Capital Airport in Grand Traverse County. The station has the search and rescue responsibility for roughly the northern and western half of the Great Lakes. In addition to operations in Traverse City, it supplies manpower and a helicopter to the Coast Guard's Air Facility Waukegan in Wisconsin during the summer months.

The Air Station operated small fixed-wing search and rescue aircraft for much of the 1970s and early 1980s. Since 1986, it has been a helicopter-only operation and today operates five MH-65C Dolphin helicopters.

Among its many notable operations over the years: a baby boy was delivered aboard one of its helicopters in 1986 and, in that same year, a Traverse City helicopter and crew was sent to Florida to assist in the recovery operations of the destroyed space shuttle Challenger.

The station maintains 24-hour operations with an assigned crew of just under 150 personnel.

Chapter 3

A B-24 Liberator–built at the Willow Run Plant in Ypsilanti–is seen at the Alpena Army Air Field during World War II. During the war, the base was used for a variety of purposes, including the testing of various B-24 modifications. (U.S. Army)

Phelps Collins (U.S. Army)

Aircraft from the First Pursuit Group operate at Alpena in this undated photo, likely taken just prior to U.S. entry into World War II. (U.S. Army)

Name: Alpena Combat Readiness Training Center. Previously, Phelps Collins Field, later Alpena Army Auxiliary Air Field, Alpena Army Air Field

Location: Alpena (Alpena County)

Established: 1931

Disposition: Still in use.

Owners: U.S.

Interesting fact: Originally named for first U.S. pilot to die in combat while flying for a U.S. unit in World War I.

Located just west of the city of Alpena, Phelps Collins Field at the Alpena Combat Readiness Training Center is staffed by a small cadre of military personnel and offers a wide range of facilities for National Guard and other military, homeland security, law enforcement and fire department personnel. Among the services offered at the base is an Air National Guard Medical Readiness Training School.

The base shares a runway with the Alpena County Regional Airport. No military aircraft are regularly assigned to the base.

Rather, outside units come to the base and utilize it as a training center, generally for no more than two weeks at a time.

After a couple years of planning and preparation work, the air field was formally opened on Aug. 31, 1931, and named in honor of Capt. Phelps Collins, a U.S. Army Air Service pilot from Alpena who was the first U.S. airman to die in combat while flying with a U.S. Army flying squadron in World War I. (Collins, like many other Americans, had originally flown in the war in a French unit known as the Lafayette Escadrille. Several U.S. pilots gave their life while flying with the Escadrille, but Collins was the first to do so flying with a U.S. unit.) Michigan Gov. Wilber M. Brucker flew into the airport for the 1931 ceremony and accepted the airport on behalf of the state. Collins Field thus became the first state-owned airport in Michigan. The field's first structure, a hangar, was built in 1935-37.

By the mid-1930s, the First Pursuit Group, stationed at Selfridge Field (see page 168), began using Alpena as a training site, beginning the long history of military training operations in Alpena. With the opening of World War II, training activity on the base increased greatly and the airfield was taken over by the Army. After a series of improvements to the runways and the building of barracks for up to 2,000 soldiers, the field became Alpena Auxiliary Army Air Field and then, on April 19, 1943, the Alpena Army Airfield. The base was operated by the 4250th Army Air Force Base Unit. During the war, the field was primarily attached to the Air Transport Command as a training base for long-range transport pilots. Other activities took place there as well, including the testing of a variety of modifications for P-47 Thunderbolt fighter aircraft. During the war, the base was also the regional headquarters for Kinross Army Airfield (later Kinchloe Air Force Base) and Raco Army Airfield (see pages 138 and 151), both in the Eastern Upper Peninsula. Later in the war, it was also a testing and training center for B-24 Liberator bombers that were built at the Willow Run Plant (see page 198) in Ypsilanti.

After World War II, the Army mostly left the base and most of the buildings on the base were torn down or auctioned off. Some of the buildings were moved into Alpena and used as houses.

In 1954, the Air Force's Air Defense Command established Alpena Air Force Station at the base, operated by the 677th Aircraft Control and Warning Squadron. The station was a radar warning location, designed to protect the industrial sites of Michigan. By 1957, the radar site operation was discontinued.

Throughout the various changes, the base continued to be operated as a training facility for the Air National Guard and other military units. Among the key facilities operated by the base, though it is actually located as part of the Camp Grayling property (see page 34) several dozen miles to the southeast, is the Grayling Air Gunnery Range, where aircraft can fire live ordnance at ground targets. Other facilities on the base in Alpena County include an urban assault training compound and an extensive aircraft fire and crash simulator.

Chapter 4

Name: Big Bay Firing Range
Location: Big Bay (Marquette County)
Established: 1952
Disposition: Closed 1953. Property now controlled by U.S. Coast Guard
Owners: U.S.

A training range for anti-aircraft artillery was operated by the Michigan National Guard at Big Bay Point in Marquette County in 1952 and 1953. A lighthouse serving shipping on Lake Superior is on the grounds and the property is now controlled by the U.S. Coast Guard.

Chapter 5

The exterior of the Brodhead Naval Armory, on Jefferson near the MacArthur Bridge, which connects Belle Isle to the rest of Detroit. (U.S. Marine Corps)

Name: Brodhead Naval Armory / Detroit Naval Armory
Location: Detroit (Wayne County)
Established: 1930
Disposition: Turned over to city of Detroit in 2005
Owners: U.S.
Interesting fact: May have the largest collection of Art Deco / Great Depression-era murals in the state.

Established as the home of the defunct Michigan Naval Militia, the Detroit Naval Armory was later home to units of the U.S. Naval Reserve and the U.S. Marine Corps Reserve.

The Michigan Naval Militia was created in 1893 and was, for the most part, a recreational and civic organization for Detroiters who owned yachts and other large pleasure craft. In the early years, the naval militia was known by such names as the "millionaire's militia." Despite the recreational nature of the organization, sailors from the militia did serve with the U.S. Navy during both the Spanish-America War and World War I. In 1915, just before the U.S. entered World War I, the U.S. Navy officially chartered the U.S. Naval Reserve and most state naval militias eventually folded into the Naval Reserve, as did Michigan's, and/or faded away.

In the 1920s, several hundred men served in the Naval Reserve in Detroit and the need was seen for a suitable, permanent facility for both Navy and Marine Corps Reservists in the area. The armory was built in 1930, at a cost of $375,000. The armory is located near the foot of the MacArthur Bridge, which connects Belle Isle in the Detroit River with the mainland. The armory was named in honor of Capt. Richard Thornton Brodhead, who was a commander of the local Naval Reserve and the prime advocate of the building of the new facility. Thornton Brodhead served for more than 40 years of combined service in the Michigan Naval Militia, the Naval Reserve and the regular U.S. Navy. For more on Capt. Brodhead, see Page 232.

The facility was used for a wide variety of both military and community purposes over the years. Perhaps most notable among the non-military activities at the armory was the first professional fight of future heavyweight boxing champion Joe Louis, in 1932. The building is also known for its extensive Art Deco art work. With the onset of the Great Depression just as the building was opening, the federal Works Progress Administration financed a large number of artistic additions inside the armory, including three large murals. It is said that the armory contains the largest collection of Depression era artwork of any building in Michigan.

From its beginnings, the building was home to a full range of military functions. During World War II, the armory was used as a training center for Navy mechanics and electricians. The building remained in use through the middle 2000s, with the headquarters company of the 1st Battalion, 24th Regiment of the Marines, an infantry unit, the last unit to remain at Brodhead. The company relocated to Selfridge Air National Guard Base (see page 168) in 2004. The building is no longer in active use by any military unit. It was turned over to the city of Detroit in 2005 and has been essentially vacant since then.

Chapter 6

The unit emblem of the 665 Air Defense Group.

Name: Calumet Air Force Station
Location: Calumet (Houghton County)
Established: 1951
Disposition: Closed Sept. 30, 1988. Abandoned.
Owners: U.S.
Interesting fact: One of several radar facilities across the state during the Cold War era.

Located in a remote area of the Keweenaw Peninsula, Calumet Air Force Station was one of about a half dozen remote radar facilities that existed around the state during the Cold War era. The function of the station was to detect possible intrusions by enemy aircraft and then to guide U.S. interceptor aircraft to the enemy's location. During most of the station's years of operation, it was operated by the 665th Radar Squadron and/or the 665th Air Defense Group.

The station was located on Mount Horace Greely, near the small town of Phoenix. Construction began on the station in July 1950 and the station's radar system became operational on May 1, 1951. The station closed in 1988 and was turned over to the Federal Aviation Administration. Prior to closing, Calumet was, along with Port Austin Air Force Station, the last active Air Force Station in Michigan. For a time after its closing, some of the

Calumet station's facilities were used as a boys' reform school. Most of the station's buildings are still standing.

Chapter 7

Col. Thomas W.B. Stockton of Flint, commander
of the Sixteenth Michigan Infantry during the Civil
War. (Library of Congress)

Name: Camp Backus
Location: Detroit (Wayne County)
Established: 1861
Disposition: Unknown
Owners: U.S.
Interesting fact: Existed for only a few weeks in 1861.

Camp Backus was a temporary site used only as the mustering-in camp for the Sixteenth Michigan, a regiment of infantry created for service in the Union Army during the Civil War. Known as Stockton's Independent Brigade, the regiment of 761 men was commanded by Col. Thomas W.B. Stockton of Flint.

The regiment left Detroit for the Washington, D.C. area on Sept. 16, 1861. The camp was disbanded with the departure of the regiment. The exact location of the camp, which existed for only a couple of weeks, is uncertain.

The following historical marker is at Stockton's home in Flint:

Thomas Stockton and his wife, Maria, were among Flint's prominent early residents. Maria, the daughter of Jacob Smith--considered to be Flint's first white settler--led the formation of the city's Ladies Library Association in 1851. An 1827 graduate of the U.S. Military Academy at West Point, Thomas Stockton (1805 - 1890) spent much of his military career as a topographical engineer in the Midwest. In 1834 he laid out the turnpike that connected Detroit and Saginaw. As a colonel he raised the First Michigan Infantry Regiment to fight in the Mexican War and Stockton's Independent Regiment (the Sixteenth Michigan) in the Civil War. Captured at Gaines Mill, Virginia, in June 1862, he was held at Libby Prison for two months. Stockton left the army in 1863 and settled permanently in Flint.

Chapter 8

Name: Camp Banks
Location: Detroit (Wayne County)
Established: 1862
Disposition: Unknown
Owners: U.S.

The location of Camp Banks has been lost to time. It existed for only a few weeks in 1862 in Detroit as a muster location during the Civil War.

Chapter 9

Units assemble in formation at Camp Blair. It is possible that the formation was called together on or about April 16, 1865, to announce the death of President Abraham Lincoln by an assassin's bullet. The large U.S. flag in the rear of the photo is at half staff. (U.S. Army)

Soldiers stand in front of the post hospital at

Camp Blair, circa 1865. (State of Michigan)

Name: Camp Blair
Location: Jackson (Jackson County)
Established: 1864
Disposition: Closed 1866. Site is now privately owned.
Owners: U.S.
Interesting fact: Remained open after Civil War to muster out thousands of Union soldiers returning home to Michigan.
Web site:www.austinblaircamp7.com

Named for Michigan Civil War Gov. Austin Blair, who lived in Jackson, Camp Blair was created to muster in and later to muster out thousands of soldiers for the Union Army. The camp was on 22 acres of land and featured about two dozen wooden buildings constructed for military use, including a 100-bed post hospital. The main entrance to the camp was on Wildwood Ave. in Jackson. During the war, the camp was under the command of Col. Grover Wormer.

After the close of fighting during the Civil War, the camp entered its busiest phase. During one two-month period in early 1865, some 7,500 troops passed through the camp to receive their final pay and to muster out of the Army. Mount Evergreen Cemetery in Jackson has a section dedicated to those soldiers who died while at Camp Blair.

After the camp was closed, the camp's property reverted to Daniel B. Hubbard, a Jackson resident who had leased the property to the Army for the duration of the war.

For more on Austin Blair, see Page 227.

Text of the Michigan state historical marker at the former camp site:

Camp Blair, during the American Civil War (1861-1865) one of Michigan's military headquarters was in Jackson. Camp Blair was planned 1863 as a draft rendezvous point and as a center for convalescing troops. Named for incumbent gover-

nor Austin Blair, a Jackson resident. It was built on this site to house 2,500 soldiers. The 11-arce camp comprised offices, a hospital, barracks, and store-houses. The first troops arrived during the spring of 1864. In the year following the war, over 22,000 Michigan troops returned home via Camp Blair. The June 27, 1866, Jackson Weekly Citizen reported demolition at the camp started: "It will only be remembered among the histories of the Great Rebellion." The location of Camp Blair was lost until members of Sons of Union Veterans researched he site 2006.

Chapter 10

Name: Camp Butler
Location: Mount Clemens (Macomb County)
Established: 1861
Disposition: Abandoned 1865
Owners: U.S.

Located in Mt. Clemens, Camp Butler was an American Civil War training and mustering camp from 1861–1865. A similar Camp Butler, also used as a Civil War mustering camp, existed in Illinois. A Camp Butler also existed in Virginia during the war.

Chapter 11

Soldiers wash their mess equipment at Camp Eaton in 1898.
(Michigan National Guard)

Name: Camp Eaton
Location: Brighton (Livingston County)
Established: 1898
Disposition: Closed after 1900. Now a state recreation area.
Owners: U.S.
Interesting fact: The only "permanent" facility created in Michigan for the mustering of troops for the Spanish-American War.

Camp Eaton is unique among Michigan's military facilities in that it was the only more-or-less "permanent" facility created in response to the Spanish-American War. Various companies of volunteers for military service were formed around the state and ordered to gather together at Camp Eaton, not far from Brighton. The land that was the camp is today part of the Island Lake Recreation Area, a state park. The camp was named for Gen.

Charles L. Eaton, who died in 1895 while serving as the adjutant general of Michigan (the top general in the state National Guard).

The U.S. declared war against Spain on April 25, 1898, and Camp Eaton was established, in name at least, the next day. In reality, the camp didn't get set up until the middle of June, when the various companies of volunteers began arriving at the camp to muster in and to be known as the First Regiment Michigan Volunteer Reserve Infantry and later as the 35th Michigan Infantry. On July 1, Col. Edwin M. Irish arrived to take command of the regiment, which consisted of 1,328 men. The Spanish-American War only lasted about three and a half months and the war was actually over before the 35th ever left Camp Eaton. The regiment served on active duty in Pennsylvania and Georgia for almost a year and then returned home.

In 1900, the camp was used as the site of an annual encampment training session for the Michigan National Guard. Shortly thereafter, and exact records are murky, the camp was disbanded and eventually set aside as a recreation area owned and operated by the state.

Here is the text of an historical marker found in Brighton:

Spanish American War Regiments

This was once the summer camp of Michigan's National Guard. Here in 1898 the five regiments which were recruited in the state during the war with Spain were organized. Ten men volunteered for everyone who could be accepted. Two of the units, the 33rd and 34th Michigan Infantry, saw action in Cuba during June and July, 1898, in the fighting around Santiago. The 31st Regiment served in the occupation of Cuba. The 32nd and 35th remained in the United States. Of the nearly 6,700 men who served in these regiments, 250 were fatalities. Most of these deaths resulted from disease, not battle action.

Chapter 12

The soldiers from the 119th Field Artillery Regiment, Michigan National Guard, fire a salute during the 100th anniversary events at Camp Grayling in June 2013. (Michigan National Guard)

Red Arrow at War painting by Michael Gnatek.

The 32nd Infantry Division, known as the "Red Arrow" Division and made up of units from the Michigan and Wisconsin National Guards, was mobilized on Oct. 15, 1940. Slated to depart for Northern Ireland after World War II began, the division was diverted to the Pacific at the last minute, arriving in Australia in May 1942. Elements moved to Port Moresby, New Guinea, in September 1942, in order to halt the Japanese invasion which threatened Australia. The Red Arrow's 126th Infantry Regiment went by ship; the 128th Infantry was airlifted in the first mass troop movement by air in World War II. Joining the Australians, the 32nd entered combat on Nov. 16, 1942. The allied forces were to take heavily-fortified Japanese positions at Buna, on New Guinea's southeast coast. It proved to be one of the most difficult campaigns of the war. Fighting in the hot, steamy jungles, the 32nd was desperately short of basic equipment, weapons, medicine and even food. In the terrible heat and drenching rain, the men of the 32nd-- many burning with fever, had to reduce Japanese positions one at a time, usually by rushing them with grenades. Most of the Japanese fought to the death but, finally, on Jan 2, 1943, Buna fell. It was the Japanese army's first defeat in modern history, but for the 32nd

Division the cost was high: 1,954 were either killed or wounded, with 2,952 hospitalized due to disease. After Buna, the 32nd participated in the long campaign to drive the Japanese from the rest of New Guinea, and went on to see heavy fighting in the Philippines. Today, the 32nd Infantry Brigade, Wisconsin Army National Guard, continues to maintain the Red Arrow heritage. (Image and information from U.S. National Guard Heritage Collection)

Name: Camp Grayling
Location: Grayling (Crawford County)
Established: 1913
Disposition: Still in use
Owners: U.S.
Interesting fact: Largest National Guard training center in the nation.

Sprawling over parts of three counties, Camp Grayling is the largest National Guard training facility in the nation. The installation, which has been home to hundreds of thousands of soldiers and others for summer training camps over the years, marked its 100th anniversary in 2013. Situated on 147,000 acres mostly in Crawford County and stretching into Otsego and Kalkaska counties, the camp provides a wide variety of settings for infantry, tank, artillery and other types of units. The camp also includes an expansive air-to-ground gunnery and bombing range for aircraft and the Grayling Army Airfield, which is primarily used by helicopters, but can accommodate some types of military cargo aircraft.

Camp Grayling was founded May 2, 1913, utilizing an initial grant of land to the state by Grayling-area lumber baron Rasmus Hanson. The facility was briefly named Camp Ferris, in honor of Michigan Gov. Woodbridge Ferris, but the name was quickly changed to reflect the name of the nearby town of Grayling. The property was added to significantly over the years. The facility has always been a National Guard training range and was never operated by the active U.S. Army, although a wide variety of troops, not just Michigan Army National Guard, train at the base regularly, including periodic foreign military teams working with U.S. forces. The camp and the city of Grayling are named after a type of fish that can be found in the area, which is a hotbed for fishermen on the AuSable River and other locals waters. Significant swathes of military-owned property are open to use by local sportsmen for hunting and fishing when not in active military use.

While the sprawling camp is typically visited by 2,000 or more military personnel for training purposes throughout the year, fewer than 200 people are assigned to the base on a full-time basis.

Two state historical markers are posted at Camp Grayling:

32nd Red Arrow Division

After American entry into World War I in 1917, President Woodrow Wilson ordered all of Michigan's National Guard to Camp Grayling. Eight thousand of these troops then went to Texas where they joined Wisconsin soldiers to form the 32nd Division. Arriving in France in 1918 the division earned the name "Red Arrow" for its swift assaults through German lines. During World War II the 32nd Red Arrow Division fought courageously in the Pacific Theatre and received a commendation from General Douglas MacArthur.

Officer's Club

The Camp Grayling Officer's Club and the land on which it is constructed were given to the state of Michigan by Rasmus Hanson, a successful Grayling businessman who made his fortune in the white pine forests. In 1913 he also donated 13,760 acres of land for the training of the militia which became known as the Hanson Grant. The Officer's Club, built in 1917, has since served as the focal point for the social and formal functions of the Michigan National Guard Officer Corps. Reminiscent of the architecture that is typical of south-

ern military structures, the colonnaded veranda and symmet-rically spaced dormers set into the low hipped roof are com-mon to militia camps and army posts erected at the turn of the century.

Chapter 13

Name: Camp Hogan
Location: Colon (St. Joseph County)
Established: 1832
Disposition: Abandoned 1832
Owners: U.S.
Interesting fact: Believed to be the eastern-most fort constructed due to the Black Hawk War

Abandoned just three days after it was constructed, Fort Hogan was named for the farmer, Daniel Hogan, who donated the land for the fort. The fort was built in 1832 by local militia and featured an earthwork palisade. The militia was led by a Captain Powers. The fort was created due to fears that the local Pottawattamie tribe would join the cause of a coalition of tribes under the leadership of a Sauk chief named Black Hawk. Black Hawk and most of his forces were centered in Illinois.

Apparently, despite the initial fears, local concerns quickly eased and it is uncertain if the fort was ever completed. No trace of the fort remains.

Chapter 14

Name: Camp Lyon
Location: Detroit (Wayne County)
Established: Aug. 21, 1861
Disposition: Closed Sept. 29, 1861
Owners: U.S.
Interesting fact: Muster site for First Michigan Cavalry

Camp Lyon was an open field near the Detroit home of Col. Thornton F. Brodhead, who was the commanding officer of the First Michigan Regiment Cavalry. The regiment began to form on Aug. 21, 1861, and officially mustered in on Sept. 13, 1861. On Sept. 29, 1861, the regiment of 1,144 men left the camp for Washington, D.C. to serve in the Civil War. The camp was disbanded with the departure of the regiment.

For more on Col. Brodhead, see Page 232.

Chapter 15

Name: Camp Smith
Location: Battle Creek (Calhoun County)
Established: 1898
Disposition: Unknown
Owners: U.S.

Camp Smith was a temporary facility near Battle Creek, likely created as a muster location for the Spanish-American War. It likely existed only for a few weeks in 1898 as a local company of soldiers formed and then the camp was disbanded when the company departed for Camp Eaton (see page 32) to join the rest of the First Michigan Regiment.

Chapter 16

Col. John Stockton served in the War of 1812 as a junior officer, then commanded the 8th Michigan Cavalry during the Civil War. The 8th Michigan organized at Camp Stockton, Mount Clemens. (Macomb County Historical Commission)

Name: Camp Stockton
Location: Mount Clemens (Macomb County)
Established: 1862
Disposition: Abandoned 1863 or 1864
Owners: U.S.

John Stockton was an early pioneer in Mount Clemens and is believed to have been the first person to build a permanent building in what is now the city. Stockton arrived in Mount Clemens in 1817, a year before the area was named Mount Clemens in honor of another early pioneer, Christian Clemens. Stockton served as the community's first postmaster.

In 1862, Stockton became a colonel and was named to head the new 8th Michigan Cavalry, which was forming for service in the Civil War. A 12-acre site in Mount Clemens was named in honor of Stockton and over 900 new recruits filed into the camp to organize the new cavalry regiment. The 8th Cavalry departed for service with the Union Army in early 1863. The camp was also used for the formation of several other cavalry units that served with various Union regiments during the war.

The camp was located between Robertson Street and the Clinton River--centered around Belleview Street. The camp was abandoned in late 1863 or possibly early 1864. The Colonial Hotel was later located on the grounds of the former camp.

After the war, Stockton was active in the civic life of Mount Clemens until his death, in Mount Clemens, on Nov. 27, 1878.

Chapter 17

A soldier from the 1st Michigan Colored Infantry, later known as the 102nd U.S. Colored Troops. The unit was one of many all-Black units to serve the Union cause during the Civil War. (Library of Congress)

Name: Camp Ward
Location: Detroit (Wayne County)
Established: 1863
Disposition: Disestablished 1864. Site was later used as elementary school.
Owners: U.S.
Interesting fact: Home of the First Michigan Colored Regiment

Camp Ward was one of many temporary mustering points for regiments that formed to serve in the Civil War. Ward was unique in that it was the mustering point for a "Colored" regiment. Shortly after the opening of the war, the Detroit Tribune and Advertiser newspaper–which served the "Colored" community, as Black Americans were known at the time–began advocating for the creation of a Colored regiment in Michigan. When U.S. Secretary of War Edwin Stanton authorized the formation of such units in July 1863, the 1st Michigan Colored Infantry quickly began to form. Henry Barns, editor of the Tribune and Advertiser, was given the rank of colonel and command of the 1st Michigan Colored. The regiment had actually begun to form informally in early 1863.

The regiment organized in the summer and fall of 1863 at Camp Ward, located on a farm north of downtown Detroit, at the modern-day intersection of Macomb and Chene on Detroit's east side. How Camp Ward came by its name has been lost to time. It is possible that the farm the camp was located on was owned by the Ward family.

The 1st Michigan Colored featured an artillery, cavalry and band section. When the unit was officially mustered into federal service, on Feb.17, 1864, it was re-designated as the 102nd U.S. Colored Troops. The roughly 900-man unit left Detroit March 28, 1864, and Camp Ward ceased to exist.

The camp's site later was used as Duffield Elementary School, 1927-2010.

The Michigan Historical Marker posted at the site's location reads:

Formed from August through October 1863, a year of draft riots and protests against the war, this Negro regiment consisted entirely of volunteers. During training, a regimental band was formed and toured southern Michigan to recruit additional volunteers. Mustered here as the 102nd U.S. Colored Troops, February 17, 1864, the 900-man unit left Detroit March 28, 1864 for service in South Carolina, Georgia, and Florida. More than 1,400 men served in the regiment during 19 months in the field; ten percent of this number died in service. The regiment was disbanded in October 1865, in Detroit.

Chapter 18

Col. Dwight A. Woodbury, commander of the Fourth Michigan Regiment Infantry, which mustered at Camp Williams. (Library of Congress)

Name: Camp Williams
Location: Adrian (Lenawee County)

Established: 1861
Disposition: Part of the Adrian College campus
Owners: U.S.
Interesting fact: One of the camp buildings was used as an Adrian College classroom building for about 100 years.

Camp Williams was a Civil War mustering site used for several weeks in the summer of 1861. The Fourth Michigan Regiment Infantry organized at the camp and the regiment's 1,025 soldiers officially mustered in to service on June 20, 1861, with Col. Dwight A. Woodbury commanding.

The camp was centered around North Hall, one of the original buildings of Adrian College, located in the small city of the same name. The people of the city quickly raised funds to build a mess hall and related facilities to make up the camp.

On June 21, nearly 30,000 people, according to contemporary news estimates, gathered to watch the Fourth march off to join the Union Army.

After the departure of the Fourth the camp returned to college use. The existing North Hall on the campus was built in the early 1970s, replacing the original Civil War-era building.

Here is the text of the Michigan historical marker at Camp Williams:

Camp Williams, Adrian

At the outbreak of the Civil War in early 1861, the trustees of Adrian College offered the use of campus buildings and grounds to the Fourth Michigan Volunteer Infantry for training. This became known as Camp Williams. The city of Adrian donated money to build a mess and dining hall. By early June ten companies of the Fourth had arrived and started their training. 1,025 soldiers came from Adrian, Ann Arbor, Dexter, Jonesville, Hudson, Sturgis, Monroe, Hillsdale, Tecumseh, and Trenton. On June 21 nearly 30,000 people came to town to see the Fourth depart for Washington. The ladies of Adrian presented Colonel Dwight Woodbury with the regimental flag. Sewn into the flag was "The Ladies of Adrian to the Fourth regiment Defend It."

Fourth Michigan Volunteer Infantry (opposite side of above)

In spring 1861 the Fourth Michigan Volunteer Infantry departed Adrians' Camp Williams for service in the Civil War. The regiment was assigned to the Army of the Potomac and saw action in forty one engagements, including Gaines Mills, Fredericksburg, Chancellorsville, and Petersburg. The Fourth was one of the few regiments to lose more men in battle than from disease. Out of 1,399 men, 307 died from May 1862 through June 1864. Three colonels died in battle defending their regimental flag: Dwight Woodbury, at Malvern Hill, Virginia; Harrison Jeffords in The Wheatfield at Gettysburg; and George Lumbard at The Wilderness, Virginia. In 1864 the reorganized Fourth trained here, at Camp Williams, once more.

Chapter 19

The unit emblem of the 781st Aircraft Control and Warning Squadron.

Name: Custer Air Force Station
Location: Battle Creek (Calhoun County)
Established: 1951
Disposition: Closed 1965. Site used for a variety of government and private uses
Owners: U.S.
Interesting fact: One of several radar facilities across the state during the Cold War era.

Located on the grounds of Fort Custer in Battle Creek, construction of Custer Air Force Station began in 1951, one of several Air Force radar stations opened in response to the Korean War and growing Cold War tensions. The 781st Aircraft Control and Warning Squadron, which was later re-designated as the 781st

Radar Squadron, began operations at the facility on April 18, 1953.

The station was short-lived; in operation only through 1965. Several of the buildings used at the station still exist and some remain used for governmental/military functions.

Chapter 20

The Commandant's Quarters of the former Detroit Arsenal in Dearborn now serves as the home of the Dearborn Historical Museum. (State of Michigan)

Henry Dearborn (U.S. Army)

Name: Detroit Arsenal
Location: Dearborn (Wayne County)

Established: 1833

Disposition: Closed as an arsenal in 1877. Buildings sold to various concerns. The Arsenal's Commandant's House is the home of the Dearborn Historical Museum.

Owners: U.S.

Interesting fact: The Arsenal's first commander suggested the name of the city, Dearborn. First of two locations named Detroit Arsenal, neither of which are in the city limits of Detroit.

By 1830, the community of Detroit had a population of well over 2,000 people and was entering a decade of significant population growth. City and military leaders decided with the growth of the city, it would be a good idea to move the bulk of the gunpowder and other explosives from the city's fort to a location outside of the city proper. A suitable location was scouted out near the Rouge River along the "Chicago Road," which connected Detroit to Chicago to the west. This would allow the munitions to be transported either via the river or over land in an emergency. Today, the former Chicago Road is known as Michigan Avenue in Dearborn. The original Commandant's Quarters at the Arsenal is now used as the Dearborn Historical Museum and fronts along Michigan Avenue in the city.

In July 1832, 235 acres were set aside for the Detroit Arsenal and construction began on the Arsenal in July 1833. Construction of the Arsenal's initial 11 buildings—and a surrounding 10-foot high masonry wall--was completed by 1837. It was the Arsenal's first commander, Col. Joshua Hand, who suggested naming the community that quickly grew up around the Arsenal as Dearbornville, in honor of Henry Dearborn, who was the Secretary of War for President Thomas Jefferson and had been a general in the War of Independence. The name of the town was shortened from Dearbornville to Dearborn in 1893.

The Arsenal remained in operation through 1877, when it was determined the facility was no longer needed. The Arsenal's buildings were sold for a variety of purposes. A number of the orginal buildings were moved or otherwise altered over the years and have a long and storied history of use for a wide variety of functions in Dearborn. The only building remaining in its original location and form is the Commandant's Quarters. Over the years, it served as a social hall, town hall, police station, school, newspaper office and other uses before it was acquired by the Dearborn Historical Society in 1949 for use as a museum.

The Detroit Arsenal in Dearborn was the first of two facilities to bear that name. Famed as part of the Arsenal of Democracy in World War II, the modern-day Detroit Arsenal (see page 54) continues to operate in Warren.

Here is the text of a state historical marker at the old arsenal:

Commandant's Quarters

This building was one of eleven built in 1833 for the United States Detroit Arsenal at Dearbornville. A walled compound, a 360 foot square, was erected to store military supplies on the frontier. Constructed of red brick in the Federal style, this arsenal was located on strategic Chicago Road, now Michigan Avenue. The quarters were a center for social and cultural events in Dearborn until they were closed in 1875. The Commandant's Quarters later became a fire station, police station, church, courthouse, school facility, library and meeting hall. The Dearborn Historical Commission acquired the building in 1949 and opened it as the city's Historical Museum on October 14, 1950.

Chapter 21

During World War II some 22,000 tanks were built for the U.S. Army at the Detroit Arsenal Tank Plant in Warren. This photo is likely from 1944. (U.S. Army)

Name: Detroit Arsenal (Tank Plant/TACOM)
Location: Warren (Macomb County)
Established: 1940
Disposition: Plant closed 1997. Former tank plant portion of complex privately held. Army continues to utilize Arsenal.
Owners: U.S.
Interesting fact: Every piece of equipment owned by the Army, from rifles to field kitchens, is "owned" by an Army command at the Detroit Arsenal. Second of two locations named Detroit Arsenal, neither of which are in the city limits of Detroit.

While the Detroit area in general was rightly known as the Arsenal of Democracy in World War II, the Detroit Arsenal Tank Plant in Warren was, coupled with the bomber plant at Willow Run (see page 198), a focal point of that industrial war-time might. During the war, more than 22,000 tanks were built at the massive 1-million-square-foot assembly plant located next to the Arsenal. The plant, designed by famed architect Albert Khan, began operations in 1941. The complex was originally built with the intention of allowing it to be used for military construction during the war and then peace-time manufacturing of other products after the war. Ultimately, the plant would be used for the construction of tanks from its creation through 1996 when production ceased. Today, the plant building is still in use, producing automotive components for private concerns.

Originally constructed by the defense arm of automaker Chrysler in 1940, the plant and its related 113-acre site was owned by the Army until 1952 when the plant was returned to Chrysler ownership. Chrysler built tanks at the plant from 1941 to 1983, when it sold the plant to General Dynamics, which operated it through 1996. During World War II, a number of barracks on the Arsenal grounds were used for the housing of German prisoners of war.

Adjacent to the former tank plant is the Detroit Arsenal complex. The Arsenal is an active Army installation, although only 100 or so of the more than 4,000 people who work at the Arsenal are active-duty Army personnel. The remainders are primarily Dept. of the Army civilians, who work in a variety of professional and technical capacities. An alphabet soup of acronyms from numerous Army commands operate at the Arsenal today. Key among them are the LCMC command, which "owns" and manages all Army assets; TACOM, which is responsible for the development and procurement of tanks, though no tanks are currently constructed in the Detroit area; and TARDEC, a major research & development center which often works closely with the auto industry and research universities on a variety of projects.

Here is the text of the state historical marker at the complex in Warren:

In 1940 the U.S. Army and the Chrysler Corporation hired Detroit architect Albert Kahn to design a self-contained tank plant. Kahn specialized in factories. In 1941 he designed 20 million square feet of defense plants. The first tank rolled off the assembly line at the sprawling Detroit Arsenal Tank Plant on April 24, 1941, amid cheering spectators. The December 7, 1941 attack on Pearl Harbor thrust the U.S. into the Second World War and tank workers into round-the-clock production. President Franklin Roosevelt and his wife Eleanor inspected the plant in September 1942. Two months later workers set the monthly record for all U.S. plants by producing 896 tanks. Tank production ended here in 1997.Just two decades after the end of World War I, Europe was again at war. Construction of the Detroit Arsenal Tank Plant began in 1940, before the U.S. became directly involved in the conflict. The 1941 Lend-Lease Act committed the U.S. to supplying arms to its allies. During World War II the U.S. government contracted with automakers to make tanks, trucks and planes. William Knudson, president of the General Motors Corporation, led the government's defense production effort. Capitalizing on the auto industry's mass production capabilities, he called on Chrysler Corporation president K.T. Keller to build tanks. By the war's end the arsenal built 22,234 tanks, over one quarter of the tanks produced in the U.S.

Chapter 22

Name: Detroit Barracks, also known as the Post at Detroit
Location: Detroit (Wayne County)
Established: 1830
Disposition: Abandoned 1866
Owners: U.S.
Interesting fact: Temporary facility created to bridge the gap between the closing of Fort Shelby (Fort Detroit) and the opening of Fort Wayne.

The Detroit Barracks was created as a temporary facility in 1830, three years after the abandonment and dismantling of Fort Shelby, which was also known as Fort Lernoult and Fort Detroit (see page 91). The Barracks was intended to fill the need for a military presence in Detroit until a new fort could be built. The new fort, Fort Wayne (see page 126), began construction in 1841 and opened in 1842, but the Detroit Barracks remained in use through 1866. Among the future luminaries who served at the Detroit Barracks was Lt. Ulysses S. Grant, who would later serve as the head of the Union Army during the Civil War and as president after the war. Grant was posted to the Barracks 1849-1851.

On Oct. 29, 1862, the Secretary of War, Edwin Stanton, authorized the raising of a company to be known as the Provost Guard, under the command of Capt. Erastus D. Robinson, to occupy the Barracks and to remain on duty in the city during the course of the Civil War. During the Civil War, the Barracks also served as an induction center for recruits for the Union Army.

In 1866, the Barracks were abandoned and all military operations in the city were transferred to Fort Wayne. After the closing of the Barracks, the site was used as the Nellie Leland School for Crippled Children. Today a condominium complex at 1395 Antietam Street in Detroit is on the land where the Barracks once stood.

Chapter 23

Name: Detroit Light Guard Armory, previously known as the Brush Street Armory

Location: Detroit (Wayne County)

Established: Original facility, 1897.Modern facility, 1956.

Disposition: Original destroyed by fire, 1945. Modern facility still in use.

Owners: U.S.

Interesting fact: Original armory hosted Joe Louis boxing matches and early Detroit Auto Shows

Web site: www.historicfortwaynecoalition.com

The history of the Detroit Light Guard Armory stretches back to before the Civil War. The "Detroit Light Guard," known by various unit designations over the years, has existed in one form or another since the days the local men gathered as a militia force to help the British regulars in Fort Detroit beat back Pontiac's Rebellion over the summer and fall of 1763 (the city was a part of the British Empire at the time.)

Detroit's Own, as the Light Guard became known, played roles in the Civil War, Spanish-American War, both World Wars and the Korean War. The Light Guard even lent its semi-official logo, a tiger head, to a new professional baseball team that began to play in Detroit in 1901, hence the name Detroit Tigers.

The Light Guard met in various locations around the city in the early 1800s. After the unit's service in the Union Army in the Civil War, the Light Guard met in rented rooms at the Detroit Firemen's Hall at the corner of Jefferson Avenue and Randolph Street until 1897 when the first official Detroit Light Guard Armory was built at the corner of Larned and Brush Streets. (This facility was also known as the Brush Street Armory.) In addition to the military operations at the Armory, the facility was also host to a wide variety of events, including various galas and balls; numerous boxing matches, several which featured a young slugger named Joe Louis; and several early editions of the annual Detroit

Auto Show, which has since evolved into the North American International Auto Show.

The armory on Brush Street was destroyed in a fire on April 17, 1945,--in the waning months of World War II–and the home element of the Light Guard moved into a former automobile factory at 285 Piquette Avenue in Detroit.

Groundbreaking for a new Light Guard Armory took place on June 4, 1956, at the Armory's current location at 4400 E. Eight Mile, near Ryan Road. At the time of the Armory's construction, it was said to be the Army's largest construction project since the end of World War II, 11 years earlier. The final building dedication ceremony was held on Nov. 16, 1957, the 102nd anniversary of the first time a Detroit militia had been organized under the name "Detroit Light Guard." Of the $3 million cost of the building project, approximately $138,000 came from donations from private citizens in Detroit and surrounding communities to support the project.

The Detroit Light Guard Armory remains in use as a key hub for the operations of the Michigan National Guard.

The Light Guard Armory is actually one of two Michigan National Guard Armories that exist in Detroit. The other is the Olympia Armory. The Olympia Armory takes its name from the beloved Olympia Arena, which was the home of the Detroit Red Wings hockey team from 1927-1979. The arena was demolished in 1987 and the armory was built on the same location, at the corner of Grand River and McGraw. A commemorative marker at the Armory highlights the history of the arena at the location.

For a list of current National Guard armories in Michigan, see Appendix D, page 222.

Chapter 24

Name: ELF Tower
Location: Republic (Marquette County)
Established: 1981
Disposition: Vacated by the Navy in 2004. Property being marketed by Humboldt Township for private development.
Owners: U.S.
Interesting fact: Over the years, more than 450 arrests were made of protesters at the remote location.

Question: How does one make contact with submerged submarines, armed with nuclear missiles, without letting the potential enemy know where the submarines are? Answer: ELF.

The Extremely Low Frequency–ELF–Naval Radio Transmitter Facility in remote Republic in the central Upper Peninsula, along with a similar facility in northern Wisconsin, allowed the Navy to send messages to submarines without the submarines needing to come to the surface–and risk detection. The ELF project was conceived of in 1981 and construction began in that same year. The system went operational in the late 1980s. Essentially, the system would send radio waves down into thousands of miles of granite bedrock beneath ground, which then bounced up into the ionosphere and from there dispersed around the globe, which the subs could detect under water. The transmitter in Republic included 56 miles of above ground antenna spread out on utility poles around the seven-acre site. About 35 Navy civilians worked at the site, which included 5 buildings, all of which still stand.

Over the years, the ELF Project was the site of numerous protests by those opposed to nuclear arms and those concerned about the effect the radio waves could be having on wildlife and the environment. Over three decades of periodic protests, more than 450 arrests were made.

With the development of new technology, the ELF system

was no longer needed and the system was de-activated in 2004. The property has since been turned over to Humboldt Township and is being marketed for a variety of potential private uses.

Chapter 25

Emblem of the 752nd Radar Squadron.

Name: Empire Air Force Station
Location: Empire (Leelanau County)
Established: 1950
Disposition: Closed 1978. Turned over to Federal Aviation Administration and National Park Service
Owners: U.S.
Interesting fact: One of several radar facilities across the state during the Cold War era.

The Empire station was one of several opened by the Air Force across the state in the early 1950s when the Cold War turned hot with the conflict in Korea. Operated by the 752nd Radar Squadron, the site's mission was to detect potential enemy aircraft and to guide U.S. interceptors to the enemy. The site was closed in 1978 by the Air Force and the radar equipment and core site of the station's operations was turned over to the Federal Aviation Administration. The remainder of the station's property was incorporated into the Sleeping Bear Dunes National Lakeshore, administrated by the National Park Service.

A small museum is maintained at the site of the former Air Force Station.

Chapter 26

Fort Brady Barracks, circa 1908. (Lake Superior State University)

Soldiers in formation at Fort Brady, likely in the first decade of the 20th century. (Lake Superior State University)

Philip Sheridan (U.S. Army)

Name: (New) Fort Brady, also Camp Lucas
Location: Sault Ste. Marie (Chippewa County)
Established: 1893
Disposition: Closed in 1944, sold to Michigan College of Mining and Technology
Owners: U.S.
Interesting fact: The site of New Fort Brady is now the campus of Lake Superior State University.

New Fort Brady was the second of two forts in Sault Ste. Marie to be named Fort Brady. Upon completion of the initial construction of the new fort in 1893, the garrison of the old fort moved from the old fort to the new, with no break on service. According to the historical marker at the site, the location for the new fort was personally chosen by Gen. Phil Sheridan, who was among the most successful Union generals during the Civil War and in 1883 was appointed as the commanding officer of the U.S. Army. It seems likely that the direct involvement of "Little Phil," as the general was known, in the site selection of the new fort was rather limited. The site for the new fort was selected in 1886. By that time, though Sheridan was still the Commanding General of the Army, much of his attention was focused on the establishment and operation of Yellowstone National Park. Yellowstone had become the country's first national park in 1872. Sheridan was a key player in the creation of the national park and Yellowstone was operated by the Army from the early 1880s until 1916.

The new Fort Brady's site was 74 acres in Sault Ste. Marie and after the initial construction was complete, it included 64 buildings. Fourteen of those buildings still exist, as of 2013.

Shortly after it opened, the fort was called on to provide troops to respond to civil unrest through many Midwestern cities, notably Chicago and Detroit, as a result of a massive railroad strike in 1894. Among other things, the Pullman Strike helped lead to the rise of labor unions, which gained in public popularity at least partially in response to President Grover Cleveland's decision to call out federal troops in an attempt to enforce an injunction against the striking workers.

By the time the new fort was built, border relations had stabilized in Sault Ste. Marie and direct threats from the British/Canadians on the opposite side of the St. Mary's River or from area Native American tribes were minimal. In both the Spanish-American War and World War II, large numbers of troops passed through the fort for training en route to eventual postings overseas. During World War II, the Army's 2nd Infantry Division used the fort as a site for cold weather training.

As World War II began, a number of efforts were put in place to provide for the defense of the Soo Locks in the St. Mary's River. The 100th Coast Artillery Regiment established a four-gun 90mm anti-aircraft battery near the Soo Locks and two similar batteries were operated by the Canadian Army on the Canadian side of the locks. The 100th also fielded a series of smaller weapons and 15 large searchlights for the defense of the locks. The 339th Barrage Balloon Battalion was also assigned to Fort Brady to protect the locks. For more on the Soo Locks, also see the entry for (Old) Fort Brady, page 68.

Even with World War II still raging, however, it was clear that Fort Brady was no longer a necessary military outpost. In 1944–WWII ended in the summer of 1945–the fort was declared surplus. In 1946, the property was sold to what is today known as Michigan Technological University, which used the property as the location of a new extension campus. That campus eventually grew to become today's Lake Superior State University. Today, a number of the original Fort Brady buildings, greatly renovated, are still in use by Lake State. Perhaps most notable among the existing buildings is Brady Hall, used as a residence hall on campus; the former fort post office, which houses the university president's office; and a 1903 infantry barracks building, now known as South Hall, which houses various classrooms and academic offices.

Fort Brady was briefly brought back to life during the Korean War and in the early years of the Cold War era, though under a different name. Camp Lucas, a small section of the fort property that had been used as the post hospital, was briefly reactivated during the Korean War, again to provide defense for the shipping canal and locks. The camp served as the battalion headquarters for the 8th Anti-Aircraft Artillery Battalion and a battery of 75mm Skysweeper anti-aircraft guns were placed there. Camp Lucas was in operation from 1951 to 1962, when it was abandoned for a final time.

Here is the text of the Michigan historical marker at the fort:

When Sault Ste. Marie expanded and its canal was widened, the river-front site of <u>Fort Brady</u> was abandoned for a higher, more strategic site selected by General Philip Sheridan. Work began in 1886, and the new fort opened in 1893. From this hilltop, New Fort Brady guarded the copper and iron ore enroute from the mineral regions of western Lake Superior through the St. Mary's ship Canal. Although never under attack, its troops were called up in 1894 during civil unrest, but primarily they protected the canal until the Second World War, when 15,000 soldiers were stationed here. In 1944 the National Guard assumed these responsibilities and New Fort Brady was closed. Camp Lucas, a small section of the fort was reactivated briefly during the Korean conflict.

Chapter 27

Woodcut showing the location of Fort Brady, circa 1857, taken from the May 9, 1857 edition of the Boston-based periodical Ballou's Pictorial.

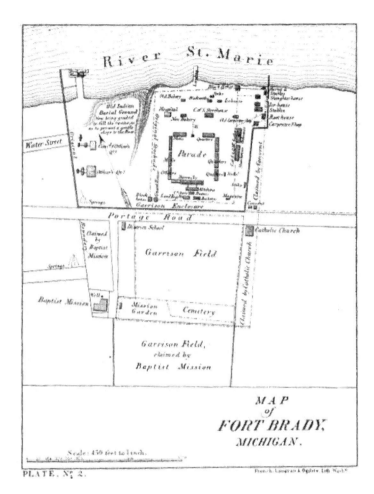

Map of Fort Brady, date unkown. (State of Michigan image)

Name: (Old) Fort Brady, also known as Post at Sault Ste. Marie, Post at St. Mary's and Cantonment Brady.

Location: Sault Ste. Marie (Chippewa County)

Established: 1822

Disposition: Closed in 1893 with opening of nearby New Fort Brady. Property was eventually sold to private owners.

Owners: U.S.

Interesting fact: Was abandoned and re-garrisoned twice

during life of fort.

Fort Brady was the name of two different forts that operated in Sault Ste. Marie. Unlike some other cities, such as Detroit, where multiple forts were built and known by different names, the move from the old fort to the new fort at Sault Ste. Marie was a continuation of the same mission, by the same garrison. There was no break in service between the closing of the first fort and the opening of the second.

Despite the signing of the Treaty of Ghent in 1814 which brought about an end to the War of 1812 between Britain and the U.S., periodic incursions by British and/or Canadian irregulars continued across the northern border on a sporadic basis. To counter this, a series of forts were built at key locations along the northern U.S. border, including the fort in Sault Ste. Marie, located just across the St. Mary's River from Sault Ste. Marie, Ontario.

With the official surrender of the Upper Michigan territory by the British after the War of 1812, the Sault Ste. Marie area returned to the control of the Chippewa nation of Native Americans. In 1820, Lewis Cass, then the territorial governor of Michigan, traveled to the Soo to negotiate with the Chippewas and reached an agreement to have the U.S. take possession of 16 square miles of land. In July 1822, American Col. Hugh Brady arrived at Sault Ste. Marie with five companies of soldiers from the 2nd Infantry Regiment to build a fort, which was later named after its first commander. Initially the fort was known as Post at Sault Ste. Marie, then as Post at St. Mary's (River) and then Cantonment Brady. Finally in 1825, the name Fort Brady was settled upon. The fort was built along the St. Mary's River, occupying just over 26 acres. The fort ran parallel to Portage Street. The fort was built on the site of the old French fort that existed in Sault Ste. Marie in 1750-1762, Fort de Repentigny (see page 117).

After the presence of the garrison at Fort Brady for several years had helped to establish a clear U.S. authority in the region, coupled with a general lessening of tensions between the U.S. and its former colonial parent -- aided by the removal of the British garrison at Fort Drummond on nearby Drummond Island in 1828 -- the need for a fort at Sault Ste. Marie began to wane. With the outbreak of the Mexican-American War in 1846, U.S. troops were needed in the South and the garrison departed Fort Brady. They were replaced at Fort Brady for the duration of the Mexican-American War by a corps of Michigan volunteers. With the conclusion of the Mexican-American War in 1848, even the volunteers left the fort and for about a year the fort was vacant. The Army eventually returned, once again garrisoning the fort beginning in the summer of 1849. In 1857, the Army again left the fort and left it empty throughout the Civil War period, not returning again until 1866.

Due to the age of the fort and its lengthy periods of inactivity, Fort Brady was falling into disrepair. However, the U.S. desired to maintain a military presence in the region, due not only to the international border there, but also to the growing importance of the Soo Locks. The first, primitive locks were built in the St. Mary's River in the 1830s. In 1870, the U.S. Army took possession of the locks on the river and began plans for a number of expansions. The authorities determined that a new fort, situated on more strategic, higher ground, was needed to adequately provide protection of the locks, a critical shipping chokepoint on the Upper Great Lakes.

Beginning in 1886, work began on a new Fort Brady in Sault Ste. Marie. In 1893, the new fort was complete and by 1894, the Army had completely left the old fort and the land was sold off in parcels to private buyers. Today, there are no remnants of the original fort remaining, though a reconstructed portion of the stockade has been built and is a tourist attraction in the area.

For more on Lewis Cass and on Hugh Brady, see Pages 235 and 231, respectively.

The site of Old Fort Brady is on both the national and state registry of historic places. Here is the text of the Michigan state historical marker:

On July 6, 1822, a battalion of American troops under Col. Hugh Brady reached the Sault, thereby reconfirming the assertion of American authority over this region made by Lewis Cass in 1820. Fort Brady was built here by year's end. The French and Indians living at the little village now recognized that this remote outpost was truly part of America. The fort was removed in 1893 to a new site chosen by General Phil Sheridan.

Chapter 28

Fort Custer is seen in this 1941 photo taken during a family day open house for the 184th Field Artillery. (Michigan National Guard)

Name: Fort Custer / Kellogg Air National Guard Base / Battle Creek Air National Guard Base
Location: Augusta (Kalamazoo/Calhoun counties)
Established: 1917 / 1940
Disposition: Still in use.
Owners: U.S.
Interesting fact: Parts of the former military reservation are now an airport, national cemetery and state recreation area.

Named for perhaps the most famed general ever to call Michigan home, George Armstrong Custer, Fort Custer was created in the summer of 1917 as Camp Custer as a training and mustering base as America prepared to enter World War I. The fort's central command area is located west of Battle Creek near the town of

Augusta. The fort's 6,000-plus acres cover parts of both Calhoun and Kalamazoo counties.

During World War I, more than 100,000 soldiers were trained at the base or otherwise passed through Camp Custer on the way to or home from World War I. Following the war, the camp continued to be used for some military purposes, including as a training center for ROTC students. It was also the site of an extensive Civilian Conservation Corps operation during the years of the Great Depression. On Aug. 17, 1940, more than a year prior to the U.S. entry into World War II, Camp Custer was re-designated as Fort Custer and was assigned use as a training complex. At the dawn of the war, the base was expanded to reach its maximum size of just over 16,000 acres, with close to 30,000 personnel assigned. During the Second World War, more than 300,000 troops took training at the base, most notably the 5th Infantry Division, which saw considerable combat action in the European campaign during the war.

During World War II, other key operations at the fort included a training school for military police; a German Prisoner of War internment center, which at one point was occupied by some 5,000 captured German military personnel; and a major Army hospital, whose notable patients included future U.S. Sen. and Republican presidential candidate Bob Dole.

In 1940, the adjacent Kellogg Army Air Field was established. The air field, which is now Battle Creek Air National Guard Base, was used as a training center for the Troop Carrier Command. The 321st Army Air Force Base Squadron was the host unit at the field during the war.

After World War II, activity at the base greatly declined and parts of the base were eventually broken off for other uses. Following the war, a Navy and Marine Corps reserve center was created at the base. Several hundred acres were detached from the base and used to create a Veterans Administration hospital and rehabilitation center. About 3,000 acres were later detached from the base for the creation of the Fort Custer Recreation Area, which is operated by the state park system and features a campground and an extensive trail system for hiking, mountain bikes and horse riders. In 1968, the Michigan National Guard assumed control of the fort's property, though much of it remains federally-owned.

Today the fort is used by numerous military units and some law enforcement agencies for a wide range of training purposes. Several Michigan Army National Guard units, including infantry, military police and medical operations, are based there

In 1947, the Kellogg Army Air Field became Kellogg Air National Guard Base and later Battle Creek Air National Guard Base. Today, that base is home to the 110th Air Wing. For many years, the 110th flew a variety of observation and attack aircraft. As of 2013, the Michigan Air National Guard at the base had begun to transition to a new mission, operating remotely piloted aerial vehicles. No aircraft of any kind are currently assigned to the base.

In the late 1990s, the Dept. of Veterans Affairs created a 700-plus acre national cemetery on the property. The cemetery–think Arlington National Cemetery on a smaller, local scale–is a beautiful and solemn place, well worth a short visit for those in the area.

Chapter 29

Name: Fort de Buade
Location: St. Ignace (Mackinac County)
Year Built: 1683
Disposition: Abandoned 1701
Owner: France
Key notes: Predecessor of Fort Michilimackinac

As with several of the very earliest forts in Michigan, some of the exact details about Fort de Buade (sometimes spelled du Buade) are difficult to determine. Fort de Buade, which may also have been known by the name Fort Michilimackinac – not to be confused with the later fort of the same name -- was certainly established by 1683 in present-day St. Ignace. Fort de Buade was the first fort built in the Upper Peninsula, except, possibly, Fort Ignatius.

The missionary priest Father Jacques Marquette had established the Mission of St. Ignace in 1671 in St. Ignace and that mission likely was at least partially fortified in 1681 due to increasing tensions between the French and local tribes. In 1681, a chief of the Seneca tribe of Native Americans named Annanhac was killed in St. Ignace as part of an ongoing dispute amongst several tribes, in which the French had taken sides. For more on the mission at St. Ignace, see Fort Ignatius, page 89.

In 1683, a French governor ordered explorers Daniel Greysolon Du Luth (later the namesake of Duluth, Minn.) and Olivier Morel de La Durantaye to establish a fortified presence on the Straits of Mackinac. They accomplished that order by completely fortifying the mission at St. Ignace and garrisoning it with troops.

In 1690, Durantaye built the separate Fort de Buade in St. Ignace, in response to a new declaration of war between France and England. This was imperative as English traders had begun operating in the Straits area. In the early 1690s, the fort was used as a launching post for various raids and attacks against the Seneca tribe, which were allied with the British. Operating from de Buade, Durantaye served as the commander for French outposts in Illinois, Ontario and the trading region in Wisconsin.

In 1694, Durantaye, who was said to have been a scrupulously honest man, was replaced as commander of the fort by Antoine de la Mothe Cadillac. The new commander apparently did not share Durantaye's ethics. Cadillac was active in the trade scene and was said to be taking a cut of most trades for himself and was accused many times of actively encouraging the sale of liquor – the trade of which he controlled – to the area tribes. Cadillac's business dealings brought him into repeated conflicts with the priests who continued to work at the local mission.

In 1701, Cadillac asked for and received permission from Paris to establish a new trading center on the Detroit River. Cadillac reasoned that he would be better able to interdict the British trade activity in the region at a location lower on the Great Lakes.

Cadillac moved his garrison to present day Detroit in 1701. It is unclear if the soldiers destroyed Fort de Buade as they departed the Straits region or if they just left it to eventually fall into ruin.

The exact location of the 1690-1701 fort has never been established. No remains of the fort have ever been found (as of summer 2013). With Fort de Buade in garrison for more than a decade, it was the first fort built in Michigan to be in "permanent" use for any significant length of time.

Just over a dozen years after Fort de Buade was abandoned, the French returned a military presence to the Straits area, with the 1715 building of Fort Michilimackinac on the southern shore of the Straits in Mackinaw City.

Here is the text from the state of Michigan historical marker for Fort de Buade:

"This fort was built by the French near here within a decade after Marquette had established his mission in 1671. Its name is that of the family of Frontenac, the French Governor of North America. Until Detroit was founded in 1701, this was

the most important French post west of Montreal. The fort's commandant had charge of all other French forts in the West. Also known as Fort Michilimackinac, it was the first of three forts which were to bear this name in the Straits area."

Chapter 30

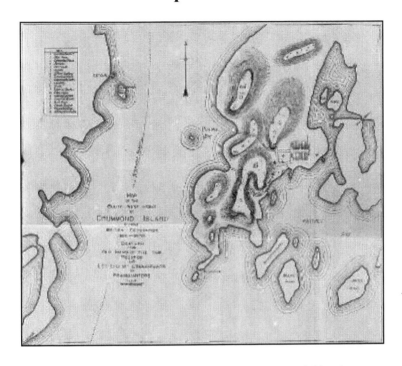

Map of the Fort Drummond area, 1898. (State of Michigan)

Name: Fort Drummond, also known as Fort Colyer or Fort Collier

Location: Drummond Island (Chippewa County)

Established: 1815

Disposition: Abandoned in 1828. Destroyed by forest fire, year uncertain.

Owners: British

Interesting fact: The last British fort on U.S. soil.

It is believed that the Fort on Drummond Island was the last foreign military or civilian outpost to be established on U.S.-owned soil.

As British forces were leaving Mackinac Island in 1815 due to the American victory in the War of 1812, the British didn't want to completely abandon the area. The fur trade was still a hugely profitable enterprise and the British wanted to be able to still exert some degree of influence over the trade. While the War of 1812 gave control of Michigan to the U.S., savvy British Army commanders of the time likely could easily envision a scenario where Michigan and the Great Lakes area might once again come under British control.

As the British departed Mackinac Island, the British established a fort on Drummond Island off the eastern coast of the Upper Peninsula in Lake Superior. While the island is clearly on the U.S. side of the border on modern maps, exactly to which nation the island belonged–and the location of the new international border as it crossed through the waters of Lake Superior--was still somewhat clouded at that point. It is also highly possible that British commanders decided to take a favorable interpretation of exactly where the border line should be drawn.

As the British forces left Fort Mackinac, their commander, Lieutenant Colonel Robert McDonall, landed them on Drummond Island and commenced the building of a fort, known varyingly as Fort Drummond, Fort Colyer or Fort Collier. The project was equal part fort and civilian community, as all the loyal British subjects who had been n Mackinac Island also re-located. The fort itself was occupied by a small garrison of soldiers, perhaps a couple of dozen, while as many as 400 people in total moved into the new settlement. The fort was located on the west end of the island.

In 1822, the determination was made that the island was actually part of the U.S., under the terms of the Treaty of Ghent, which ended the War of 1812. Even with that proclamation however, the British were slow to leave the island. They slowly began to move some equipment to a new location in Ontario. Finally, in 1828, an American force led by Lt. T. Pierce Simonton arrived to take possession of the fort on Nov. 14. In their haste to finally depart– and testament to the slowness of their departure some six years after the determination was made that the island was in fact American–a great deal of furniture and other personal possessions were left behind by the British in their haste to depart.

While the British were gone, the U.S. Army had no desire to garrison the remote fort. The fort was therefore then abandoned shortly after the arrival of the Americans. At some point in the ensuring years, the buildings and stockade were destroyed in a forest fire. A number of chimneys, wells and similar stone structures from the fort era still exist, some of which have been incorporated into homes or other buildings. Today, all of the land that constituted the fort is privately held.

Drummond Island was named for Gordon Drummond, a British military officer who became the first Canadian-born person to command the military and civil government of Canada. He served as Governor-General and Administrator of Canada, 1815-1816.

Here is the text of the Michigan state historical marker on the island:

> *Forced by the Treaty of Ghent to evacuate the fort they had captured on Mackinac Island during the War of 1812, the British selected this island as an alternate military post. The stronghold was close to the traditional Indian gathering point at the Straits of Mackinac in order to sustain English control of the Indians and the Upper Great Lakes fur trade. Built by Colonel Robert McDonall and his men, Fort Drummond and the nearby village at Collier's Harbor were maintained for more than a decade. The British abandoned their stronghold in 1828, six years after Drummond Island was ruled United States territory. Now summer cottages occupy this rocky countryside and only a few ruined chimneys survive as reminders of the conflict between British and American sovereignty in the Old Northwest.*

Chapter 31

Col. George McDougall, Jr., first lighthouse keeper at Fort Gratiot. (U.S. Army)

Lucius Lyon, oversaw construction of the Fort Gratiot Light. (Library of Congress)

Name: Fort Gratiot

Location: Port Huron (St. Clair County)

Established: 1814

Disposition: Abandoned in 1895. Part of property now used as a county park.

Owners: U.S.

Interesting fact: The adjacent Fort Gratiot Light has been in continuous use since 1825.

The name Gratiot is a familiar one in southeast Michigan, particularly as one gets closer to the lake fronts. Today, one can travel from Detroit to Port Huron on Gratiot Avenue. In 1814, U.S. Army Capt. Charles Gratiot was sent to build a fort to guard the waters where the St. Clair River meets Lake Huron in Port Huron. Gratiot built his fort on the same location as that of Fort St. Joseph, which had been used by the French for about two years in the 1680s.

Today, the town of Fort Gratiot in St. Clair County recalls the heritage of this early fort.

The fort was garrisoned by a detachment of the 2nd U.S. Infantry from 1814-22, when it was abandoned. The Army returned to the fort in 1828 and garrisoned it through 1879. Though parts of the fort were used for various intermittent federal purposes over the next 16 years, the fort was completely shut down and abandoned in 1895.

In 1825, construction began on a light house, known as the Fort Gratiot Light, on land adjacent to the fort. Construction on the light was completed in 1829.

The light's first keeper was Col. George McDougall, Jr. The light's construction was overseen by Lucius Lyon, who would later become one of the first U.S. Senators from the state of Michigan. The light was automated in 1933, but remains in active use and its operation is overseen by the Coast Guard.

Today, part of the fort's property is used for Pine Grove Park in Fort Gratiot.

For more on Charles Gratiot, see page 239.

Chapter 32

The entrance to Fort Holmes, seen in 2012.
(Mackinac State Historic Parks)

Name: Fort Holmes, previously known as Fort George
Location: Mackinac Island (Mackinac County)
Established: 1812
Disposition: Closed as fort in 1875. Maintained as an historic site by State of Michigan
Owners: British, 1812-1815; U.S., 1815-1875.
Interesting fact: One of two forts that exist on Mackinac Island

Fort Holmes is the lesser known of the two forts on Mackinac Island (the other being Fort Mackinac, page 100). Located on the opposite side of the island (Holmes is on the north, Mackinac on the south), and first known as Fort George, this fort was created in the wake of one of the most embarrassing battles of the War of 1812, from an American perspective.

During the War of 1812, British forces landed on the island on July 17, 1812, and moved on Fort Mackinac. The garrison of 60 U.S. soldiers at Fort Mackinac had no option but to surrender the fort. With the Americans off the island, the British quickly began to prepare for what they assumed would be an American counter-attack. As part of their defensive effort, the British constructed a palisade and blockhouse on the highest point on the island and dubbed it Fort George, in honor of the king.

In July 1814, five U.S. ships landed at the island, bringing U.S. forces to try to re-take the island. The attack was repulsed and the British retained control of the strategic island in the Straits of Mackinac. In the fighting, U.S. Major Andrew H. Holmes was killed on Aug. 4, 1814. The following summer, a treaty was signed between the U.S. and Britain, after a U.S. victory in the war, despite the loss of the Battle of Mackinac Island. With the treaty in hand and the war over, U.S. forces returned to the island and peacefully resumed possession of Fort Mackinac and, along with it, Fort George. The Americans renamed Fort George in honor of Holmes.(For more on the Battle of Mackinac Island, see pages 100 and 241.)

The blockhouse at Fort Holmes was allowed to fall into disre-pair and was at times used for target practice by U.S. soldiers stationed at Fort Mackinac. During the Mexican-American War and the U.S. Civil War, the island's two forts were essentially left unattended, with only one caretaker soldier assigned to care for both facilities. In 1875, Congress created Mackinac National Park, the nation's second national park after Yellowstone, and assigned soldiers to the park to care for the facilities and to act as park rangers. In 1895, Congress closed the national park at Mackinac. The property was transferred to the State of Michigan and the property became the first state park in Michigan.

The Fort Holmes blockhouse was rebuilt by the state park system in 1904, but was destroyed in a 1933 fire. It was rebuilt again in 1936, but was again destroyed by fire shortly thereafter. During the 1936 reconstruction, the fort's earthworks and a small part of the stockade were recreated and those facilities remain in place. In the summer of 2013, the Mackinac State Historic Parks announced a plan to rebuild the blockhouse again and refurbish the existing structures. The project is to be completed in time for the 200th anniversary of the 1814 Battle of Mackinac Island.

Three Michigan state historical markers are near Fort Holmes.

Battlefield of 1814, Mackinac Island

Here in this area on Aug. 4, 1814, an American force battled the British in a vain attempt to recapture the island which the British had seized at the outbreak of the War of 1812. Coming ashore at what is known as British Landing, *the Americans under Col. George Croghan soon ran into strong resistance as they advanced inland. An attempt to outflank the British line was repulsed by Indians hidden in the thick woods and resulted in the death of Maj. Andrew Holmes. Croghan withdrew when he found he could not defeat the British.*

British Landing, Mackinac Island

Here, during the night of July 16-17, 1812, a small force of British regulars and several hundred voyageurs and Indian allies from St. Joseph Island landed. They occupied a height that overlooked Fort Mackinac and demanded its surrender. Lt. Porter Hanks, commander of the American garrison of 57 soldiers, had not known that war had been declared. Realizing that resistance was hopeless and might provoke an Indian massacre, Hanks capitulated without a fight.

Fort Holmes

Here in 1812 on the island's highest point, a blockhouse and stockade were built by the British and named Fort George. It was the bulwark of British defenses in 1814 when the American attack was repulsed. After the war the Americans renamed the post in honor of Maj. Holmes who was killed during the American assault in 1814. The fort was not maintained by the Americans however. The present blockhouse is not the original building.

Chapter 33

Name: Fort Ignatius
Location: St. Ignace (Mackinac County)
Established: 1669
Disposition: 1670
Owners: France
Interesting fact: Part of the mission established by Father Jacques Marquette.

Some sources refer to the Jesuit mission established by Father Jacques Marquette in St. Ignace in 1669 as Fort Ignatius. After Marquette established the mission, some French soldiers were assigned there and they built a wooden fort. A year later, in 1670, they abandoned the fort.

If the facility built at St. Ignace was truly a bona fide "fort" it would be the earliest fort built by European powers in Michigan. If not, that honor belongs to Fort Miami in St. Joseph (see page 107), which was built about 10 years later, in 1679. See also, Fort de Buade, page 76.

Here is the text to three relevant Michigan state historical markers:

St Ignace

Pere Marquette established in 1671 the Mission of St. Ignace. *French troops soon after built* Fort Buade. *The state's second oldest white village guarded the Straits while serving as the most important French fur post in the northwest. By 1706 both the fort and mission where abandoned. Only in the 19th century did lumbering and fishing revive the town.*

St. Ignace Mission

In 1671 the mission of St. Ignace was established so that the Christian message could be brought to several thousand Indi-

ans living on this shore. The founder was Father Jacques Marquette, the Jesuit missionary. In 1673 he left on his great journey to the Mississippi Valley. He never returned to his mission before he died in 1675. Two years later his bones were reburied here beneath the chapel altar. In 1706, after French troops had abandoned the fort, the chapel was destroyed.

Mackinac Straits

Nicolet passed through the Straits in 1634 seeking a route to the Orient. Soon it became a crossroads where Indian, missionary, trapper and soldier met. From the 1600's through the War of 1812 first Frenchman and Englishman, then Briton and American fought to control this strategic waterway. In 1679 the Griffin was the first sailing vessel to ply these waters. The railroad reached the Straits in 1882. Until the Mackinac Bridge was opened in 1957, ferries linked the north and south.

Chapter 34

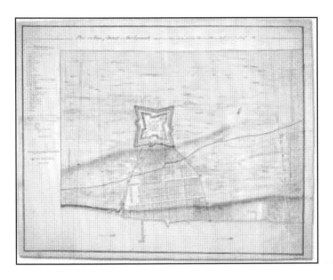

This map shows a survey of Fort Lernoult from the year 1792. (Library of Congress)

Isaac Shelby, governor of Kentucky and leader of a force of Kentucky militia who helped liberate Fort Detroit in 1813. (State of Kentucky)

Daguerreotype image of William Henry Harrison, the general who helped liberate Fort Detroit in 1813. He would later serve as the nation's ninth president. (White House)

John Hamtramck, first commander of Fort Shelby
and Namesake of Hamtramck, Mich. (U.S. Army)

Name: Fort Lernoult/Fort Shelby. Also known as Fort Detroit
Location: Detroit (Wayne County)
Established: 1779
Disposition: Transferred to city of Detroit in 1826. Dismantled in 1827.
Owners: British, 1779-1796; U.S., 1796-1812; British, 1812-1813; U.S., 1813-1826.
Interesting fact: Second of three forts built in Detroit.

One of the watershed moments in the early history of Detroit took place at this fort, the second of three built in Detroit. At varying times, the fort was known for its first commander, British Capt. Richard B. Lernoult; as Fort Detroit; and later still as Fort Shelby. It was at this fort in 1796 wherethe forces of U.S. General "Mad" Anthony Wayne took possession of the Detroit region from the

British and moved it to U.S. control. Numerous places and landmarks in the Detroit area now bear the Wayne name in his honor, perhaps most notably Wayne County, which includes the city of Detroit; Wayne State University in the city; and the Wayne County suburban city of Wayne. The fort, of which no original remains exist (though Wayne State University and other organizations own numerous artifacts), was centered at the modern intersection of Fort and Shelby streets.

In the fall of 1778, the American Revolutionary War was in full bloom, and the British held possession of the Michigan region. British Capt. Lernoult, then in command of Fort Pontchartrain/Fort Detroit (see page 111), which had been built in 1701, determined that the fortifications at the existing fort were inadequate to withstand a possible attack by advancing U.S. forces. Lernoult quickly commissioned the construction of a new, stronger fort, named Fort Lernoult in his honor.

Continental (U.S.) forces under the command of Col. Daniel Brodhead marched to within about 90 miles of Detroit, but various logistical problems beset the expedition and the attack on Ford Detroit never materialized. The British retained control of the fort and the region, despite the eventual American victory in the Revolutionary War. Finally, with the signing of the Jay Treaty several years after the conclusion of the war and Wayne's victory at Fallen Timbers in northern Ohio,the British agreed to abandon the fort in Detroit, along with five others in what was then considered the "western region." In June 1796, the British peacefully departed the fort and moved across the Detroit River to the fort in Amherstburg, Ontario. On July 11, 1796, a detachment of 65 soldiers from Gen. Wayne's Army, led by Capt. Moses Porter, took possession of Fort Detroit without a shot being fired. Col. John Hamtramck arrived two days later to take command. Wayne himself arrived several weeks later. For more on Wayne, see page 245.

The U.S. assigned a permanent garrison to the fort and, in 1805, U.S. Secretary of War Henry Dearborn ordered the fort to be renamed as Fort Detroit.

The fort was the scene of a battle in 1812 that caused the fort to fall back into British hands during the War of 1812. With the outbreak of hostilities between the U.S. and Britain, Michigan Territorial Gov. William Hull was appointed as the commanding general of the U.S. Army of the Northwest with Fort Detroit as his headquarters. In July 1812, Hull and his troops departed the fort with a plan to invade Canada, but he quickly abandoned that plan after learning that the British had captured the Upper Great Lakes stronghold of Fort Mackinac (see page 100) on Mackinac Island. In August 1812, British Gen. Isaac Brock set up an artillery battery in Windsor, Ontario, across the Detroit River from Fort Detroit. On Aug. 15, Brock sent Hull an ultimatum, demanding the Americans' surrender. Hull declined to surrender. The next morning, supported by his artillery and the cannons of two British ships in the river, Brock crossed into Detroit and began to march on the fort. Fearing a massacre at the hands of Brock's Native American allies–a threat implicit--made in Brock's ultimatum–Hull surrendered the fort. Hull would later by court-martialed and sentenced to be shot for his surrender, but was eventually pardoned by President James Madison. For more on Hull, see page 240.

The British Army controlled the fort for about a year until suffering reverses in the region as a result of a defeat in the Battle of Lake Erie. With British naval forces scattered, a U.S. force of about 1,000 soldiers, under the command of future president William Henry Harrison, marched on the fort, prompting the British to leave the fort and retreat back into Canada. The U.S. forces entered the fort on Sept. 29, 1813, and shortly thereafter named it Fort Shelby in honor of Kentucky Gov. Isaac Shelby, who was marching with Harrison and bringing a sizable regiment of Kentucky militiamen with him. (It is somewhat unclear if the change in name to Fort Shelby was ever officially recognized by the War Department.)

U.S. forces occupied the fort for about a dozen years after the re-capture, before the decision was made to abandon the fort in 1826. It was given to the city in that year and was demolished the following spring. There would be no fort in Detroit for the next 15 years–a gap partially filled by the building of the Detroit Barracks (see page 57)--until the construction of Fort Wayne (see page 126) in Detroit in 1842.

Today several commercial buildings exist on the site of the former fort, including the federal Theodore Levin U.S. Courthouse.

Several Michigan historical markers apply to the various events that took place at or near Fort Lernoult:

Hull's Trace. Brownstown Township

In April 1812, as the United States prepared for a possible war with Great Britain, Michigan's Territorial Governor William Hull, became the commander of the Army of the Northwest. His first task was to lead his army from Dayton, Ohio to Detroit, building Hulls Trace, a two hundred mile long road, as it marched. The army left Dayton on June 1. As it cut the trace through the wilderness from Urbana north, it laid logs crosswise across swampy areas to create a rough but stable corduroy roadbed that could support supply wagons. In late June, a detachment from Frenchtown commanded by Hubert Lacroix also worked on the road, attempting to follow a route laid out under an 1808 territorial Legislative Council act. On June 18, 1812, war was declared. Hulls army arrived in Detroit on July 5.

Hulls Trace, which linked Detroit and Ohio, was to be the Michigan Territories inland lifeline during the War of 1812. However, the Detroit River and Lake Erie gave the British easy access to the Michigan portion of the road. American efforts to use the road to bring supplies and men from Frenchtown, present-day Monroe, were foiled twice before Hull surrendered Detroit on August 16, 1812. After the war the Hulls Trace route was used for ever-improving roads, beginning in 1817 with a new military road. In 2000 low water levels in the Huron River revealed a quarter mile of the old corduroy road, lying three to six feet beneath Jefferson Avenue. Axe marks were visible on some of the logs. This rare example of a sur-

viving corduroy road is listed in the National Register of Historic Places.

Battle of Monguagon, Trenton, Mich

On August 9, 1812, Lieut. James Miller and a force of about 600 American regulars and militia moved down the Hull's Trace in an attempt to bring desperately needed supplies from Frenchtown (Monroe) to Detroit. A similar effort had failed at Brownstown on August 5. Near the Wyandot village of Monguagon, American scouts ran into a British and Indian force of about 400 men led by Capt. Adam Muir and Tecumseh. In the heavy fighting that followed, the Americans drove the British back through present-day Trenton and across the Detroit River, while Native forces withdrew into nearby woods. Despite this tactical victory, Miller returned empty-handed to Detroit, which American General William Hull surrendered to the British a week later.

Michigan Wayndot and Monguagon, Trenton, Mich. (opposite side of above)

The Michigan Wyandot who fought at Monguagon were neutral at the beginning of the War of 1812. In the years leading up to the war, their villages at Monguagon and Brownstown had not joined the loose coalition led by the Shawnee brothers Tenskwatawa (The Prophet) and Tecumseh in its fight against American expansion onto Indian lands. However, in early August 1812. Tecumseh and Roundhead, his leading Wyandot supporter, convinced the Wyandot and their head chief, Walk-in-the-Water, to join them and the British. The Anglo-Native alliance was repulsed, but the Wyandot villages continued to block Hull's Trace, the American's supply route from Ohio to Fort Detroit.

Battle of Brownstown, Gibraltar, Mich

In this vicinity on Aug. 5, 1812, six weeks after the outbreak of war, an Indian force, led by the famous Shawnee chief, Tecumseh, ambushed about 200 Americans under Major Thomas Van Horne who were on the way south to the River Raisin. There, supplies vitally needed by Hull's army in Detroit, were awaiting an escort through the Indian blockade of the River Road. Tecumseh opened fire as the Americans forded Brownstown Creek. Van Horne, overestimating the Indians' numbers, ordered his men to fall back. The retreat soon became a panic-stricken flight back to Fort Lernoult. Seventeen Americans were killed, 12 wounded, and two captured and murdered. One Indian was killed.

Fort Lernoult

This marks the site of the southwest bastion of Fort Lernoult. It was here, on July 11, 1796, that the American flag was first flown over Detroit. the fort was built by the British in 1778-79 to protect Detroit against possible attack by George Rogers Clark and the American army. Overlooking the stockaded village and named for its commander, Richard B. Lernoult, the fort controlled river traffic and land routes. The fort was not attacked during the American Revolution. However, it was then the foremost British military post in the West, a base for Indian raids against American frontier settlements, and a guardian of the rich fur trade. Although the peace treaty of 1783 gave Michigan to the United States, the British did not evacuate the fort until 1796. In 1812, Fort Lernoult was surrendered to the British, but was regained by the Americans in 1813 and re-named Fort Shelby. The last troops were removed in 1826. The fort was leveled in the next two or three years.

Col. John Francis Hamtramck, Hamtramck

John Francis Hamtramck was a native of Canada who dedicated his life to the new American nation. Born in 1756, Hamtramck fought in the American Revolution. He distinguished himself during and after the war fight both Indian and British forces. In 1787 he was made commander of Post Vincennes in the Illinois Territory. There Hamtramck was instrumental in negotiating a peace treaty with area Indians. In 1793 Hamtramck was named lieutenant colonel in the forces led by General Anthony Wayne. The next year, Hamtramck was cited for bravery in Wayne's victory at the Battle of Fallen Timbers. In 1796, Hamtramck, a newly appointed colonel, was further honored when he was given command of the fort at Detroit which had previously been in British hands. Except for two years, he remained there until his death in 1803. In 1798 one of the four townships of in Wayne County was named for this military hero.

War of 1812 Dead, Washington Blvd at Michigan Ave., Detroit

Hardship struck soon after American troops regained Detroit on Sept. 29, 1813, during the War of 1812. Soldiers quarters were lacking, and food supplies became desperately short. Then a disease resembling cholera broke out among the soldiers. By Dec. 1, 1813, nearly 1,300 officers and men were sick. Medical supplies were almost gone. Conditions worsened. When coffins became unobtainable, many soldiers were buried in a common grave at this site. Some 700 may have died before the epidemic ran its course.

Chapter 35

Cannon and part of the limestone wall at Fort Mackinac, as it appears today. (Mackinac State Historic Parks)

William Beaumont, post surgeon at

Fort Mackinac.

Name: Fort Mackinac
Location: Mackinac Island (Mackinac County)
Established: 1780-81
Disposition: Closed as a military fort in 1895. Now a state park
Owners: British, 1780-1796; U.S., 1796-1812; British, 1812-1815; U.S., 1815-1895
Interesting fact: One of the premier examples of 19th century military life in the Upper Great Lakes region.

In 1780, Patrick Sinclair, lieutenant governor of the Michilimackinc region, determined that Fort Michilimackinac (see page 107), in present-day Mackinaw City on the Lower Peninsula mainland, was inadequate for the needs of the British Army to maintain control of the Straits. Sinclair determined that a fort made of limestone on nearby Mackinac Island would provide him with a strategic advantage. In 1781, the British finished the fort and moved the garrison from Fort Michilimackinac to the island.

With the American victory in the Revolutionary War in 1783, Britain officially relinquished control of Upper Michigan. It wasn't until 1796, however, that a U.S. force arrived to take possession of the fort. At that time, the British left peaceably and moved to Fort St. Joseph on St. Joseph Island in the Ontario, Canada, portion of the St. Mary's River, near Sault Ste. Marie.

When the War of 1812 began in June of that year between the U.S. and Britain, British forces in Upper Canada got word of the new war before their American foes on Mackinac Island. British Gen. Isaac Brock sent a force of some 200-plus British regulars and Native American allies to attack Mackinac Island from Fort St. Joseph. The invaders landed on the opposite side of the island from the fort on July 17, 1812, and moved two cannons into place for the planned attack on the fort. The British then sent an ultimatum to the Americans in the fort. U.S. Lt. Porter Hanks was in com-.

mand of the fort with a force of about 60 men. Hanks was at a major disadvantage compared to his British foes– he had not been informed by his superiors in Detroit that a state of war existed between the U.S. and Britain. Hanks had therefore not taken any additional measures to secure his defenses. Outmanned and with the British artillery already in place, Hanks had no choice but to surrender. After the British captured the fort, they continued to flag an American flag over the fort for several days, using the subterfuge to capture several unsuspecting American ships that came into the harbor. With the fort securely in British hands, the British forces also built Fort George (later Fort Holmes) (see page 85) to bolster the defense of the island against a likely future counterattack by the Americans. In July 1814 the Americans did try to recapture the island by military force, but the assault failed miserably. (For more on the Battle of Mackinac Island, see pages 85 and 250. For more on Isaac Brock, see page 229).

Following the eventual American victory in the War of 1812, Fort Mackinac was peacefully transferred from the British back to the Americans in July 1815. With peace between the U.S. and Britain/Canada secured, Fort Mackinac was no longer needed as a front-line military post and at various points over the next several decades was all but abandoned, save for a single caretaker who was assigned to care for both Fort Mackinac and Fort Holmes.

During the period between the War of 1812 and the Civil War, several notable occurrences happened at the fort. In the summer of 1822, a fur trader by the name of Alexis St. Martin, was shot in the stomach in an accidental weapon discharge. The Fort Mackinac post surgeon, Dr. William Beaumont, responded to the emergency. With the aid of the doctor, St. Martin returned to full health, but a hole developed in his body, exposing his stomach to the outside environment. Beaumont used this development to conduct a wide range of experiments on St. Martin's digestive system (with St. Martin's consent) and wrote extensively on the results these experiments. As a result, Beaumont became known as the Father of Gastric Medicine. Beaumont's legacy is honored by a system of hospitals and health care facilities in southeast Michigan.

About a decade after Beaumont's experiments, Lewis Cass, future territorial governor of Michigan, used Fort Mackinac as the staging area for the launching of a major mission of exploration in 1832 to find the headwaters of the Mississippi River. Also in the 1830s, Indian agent Henry Schoolcraft was stationed at the fort and conducted a number of noted studies on the language and culture of the area's Native American tribes. These studies were later published and considered a baseline for future academic research on the topics. For more on Cass, see page 235.

During the Civil War, the fort was mostly vacant, though it did play a small role in that conflict. For a brief period, three Confederate prisoners were held at the fort as political prisoners, guarded by a volunteer militia.

In 1875, the Army declared Fort Mackinac as excess and the fort became the nation's second national park, after Yellowstone National Park. The Army continued to occupy the fort, though now the soldiers served as park rangers.

In 1895, the Army determined to eliminate the costs of posting soldiers at the fort and the national park was closed. The state of Michigan took possession of the fort shortly thereafter and re-opened it as a state park.

Today, Fort Mackinac is one of the iconic images of Michigan. It is visited by thousands of tourists a year who are able to visit more than a dozen fully-maintained period buildings. Re-enactors are at the fort during the summer months and provide a variety of demonstrations, including a daily firing of one of the fort's cannons, in season. Fort Mackinac is the ultimate must-see location for anyone interested in Michigan's early history.

Here is the text of the Michigan state historical marker at the fort:

Fort Mackinac

Mackinac Island has been called the most historic spot in the Middle West. Fort Mackinac was first built by the British in 1780-81. It was not until 1796, thirteen years after the end of *the Revolutionary War, that the British relinquished this fort to the Americans. At the outbreak of the War of 1812 the British seized the island and built Fort George. This fort, which you see to the north beyond the Rifle Range, was renamed <u>Fort Holmes</u> by the Americans who reoccupied the island in 1815. Troops garrisoned Fort Mackinac until 1895.*

Chapter 36

Sieur de La Salle

Name: Fort Miami
Location: St. Joseph (Berrien County)
Year Built: 1679
Disposition: Destroyed by own soldiers, 1681
Owner: France
Key notes: First fort in Michigan

The earliest military fort in Michigan was an outpost of the Kingdom of France in the modern day city of St. Joseph in the extreme southwest corner of the state.(An argument can be made that Fort Ignatius in St. Ignace was the first fort in the state, see the entry on page 89.)

In the late 1600s, the St. Joseph River was known as the Miami River, and it was from that river that Fort Miami derived its name. The fort was established in 1679 by a famed French explorer of the Great Lakes. Known in various sources as Rene-Robert Cavelier, Sieur de La Salle and Robert de La Salle, the explorer traveled extensively through what is today the U.S. and Canada and is perhaps best known for his extensive travels along the Mississippi River. He claimed the entire Mississippi River basin for France.

After traveling the Upper Great Lakes in a small sailing ship known as Le Griffon, La Salle and his men split up, so Le Griffon could take a load of furs back to the east from Green Bay Wisconsin. Meanwhile La Salle and some of his men continued south along Lake Michigan, eventually arriving at what is today St. Joseph in November 1679. By January 1680, a stockade was completed and used by La Salle as a base of operations for about a year. After a number of other travels, La Salle returned to Fort Miami in 1681 to prepare for a trip down the Mississippi River. La Salle's soldiers destroyed the fort after their 1681 departure.

Fort Miami is just one of numerous forts and other outposts created by La Salle in his treks across the country. For more on La Salle, see page 237.

A state of Michigan historical marker is posted at the site of Fort Miami, in downtown St. Joseph. It reads:

"Here in November, 1679, on the Miami River, as the St. Joseph was then called, La Salle, the French explorer, built a fort as a base for his western explorations. Here he awaited the Griffin, the upper lakes' first ship. When the ill-fated vessel did not come he made his way on foot to Canada through lower Michigan's uncharted wilderness. He returned in 1681 to prepare his great push down the Mississippi. A decade later the French built Fort St. Joseph, some 20 miles upriver near Niles."

Chapter 37

Fort Michilimackinac as it appears today, as a tourist destination for thousands of visitors every summer. (Mackinac State Historic Parks)

Name: Fort Michilimackinac
Location: Mackinaw City (Mackinac County)
Established: 1715
Disposition: Abandoned in 1781. Several of the fort's buildings were moved to Fort Mackinac and the remainder burned. In 1909, the area became Michigan's second state park. In the 1930s, the fort's stockade was re-built as an historical attraction.
Owners: French, 1715-1761; British, 1761-1781.
Interesting fact: The site of the most infamous game of lacrosse ever played.
Web site: www.mackinacparks.com

Today a part of the excellent Mackinac State Historic Parks system operated at the tip of the mitt of the Lower Peninsula, Fort Michilimackinac is visited by thousands of people every year. It, and the fort that replaced it, nearby Fort Mackinac (see page 100), are two of the iconic images of early Michigan.

By the 1660s, the French fur trade was flourishing in the Straits of Mackinac area. In the 1680s, the French built Fort de

Buade (see page 76) in modern-day St. Ignace to establish a military presence in the Straits, but that fort was in operation likely for no more than 15 years at most. Despite a number of challenges–notably dischord between the French and a number of the area Native American tribes–the fur trade was simply too profitable to be stopped, thus prompting the need for a military presence.

In 1715, the French, under the command of Constant Le Marchand de Lignery, built a wooden stockade on the south shores of the Straits, near an existing Odawa community, with whom the French were allied. This stockade, Fort Michilimackinac, would be expanded a couple of times over the years and would stand until 1781, when the fort's then-owners, the British, relocated to a new limestone-walled fort on the high ground of Mackinac Island.

From Fort Michilimackinac's earliest days, continuing through the 1760s, the French, often working with allied Native American tribes, engaged in battles with various other tribes, sometimes in the vicinity of the fort, other times as far away as Wisconsin. In 1753, more than 1,200 warriors and chiefs from 16 tribes gathered outside the fort for a council. Each of the chiefs, and fort commander Louis Lienard de Beaujeu, agreed to a peace pact and Beaujeu encouraged all of the chiefs to aggression against France's most-hated rival, the British Empire.

In 1754, just a year after the council at Michilimackinac, France and England began to engage in what eventually became a global conflict that came to be known as the Seven Years War. The North American portion of that war is known today as the French & Indian War. As a result of the British victory in the war, Britain took control of all of Upper Canada and what is today the state of Michigan, thus causing the Straits of Mackinac area to pass into British hands. In September of 1761, British Capt. Henry Balfour arrived with a contingent of troops to take possession of Fort Michilimackinac. From the very beginning tensions ran high between the new British garrison and local Native Americans, who had grown accustomed to the French at the fort.

In the spring of 1763, the Native American uprising known as Pontiac's Rebellion challenged British forts around the Great

Lakes region. Despite these high tensions, British commanders at Fort Michilimackinac planned a big celebration on June 2, 1763, in honor of King George III's birthday. As part of the celebration, local Chippewas arranged a game of baggatiway–a forerunner of the modern game of lacrosse–with a visiting group of warriors from the Sac tribe. The game was played right outside the gates of the fort and the British soldiers came out to watch and join in the festive mood. During the game, the ball was "accidentally" thrown over the fort walls and some players ran inside the fort to retrieve it. This was the pre-arranged signal for the Chippewas and Sacs to attack the unsuspecting soldiers. About half of the garrison's soldiers were killed in the attack and the remainder captured. After the Native Americans left, a group of Canadians, who were part of the British empire–occupied the fort for about a year. In September 1764, the British finally re-garrisoned the fort with two companies of regular infantry.

In the late 1770s, the British deemed Fort Michilimackinac to be inadequate. Under the command of Patrick Sinclair, lieutenant governor of the Mackinac region, a new fort was built on Mackinac Island in 1781. During the winter of 1781-82, Fort Michilimackinac was dismantled and the materials from the fort were transported over the ice to new Fort Mackinac on the island. The remains of Fort Michilimackinac that could not be moved or were not needed were eventually destroyed by the British.

The area that contained the fort eventually became a park in the new community of Mackinaw City. In 1904, the park was transferred to the state of Michigan and by 1909 the park was combined with the state park on Mackinac Island as part of the Mackinac Island State Park Commission. In the 1930s, the stockade at the fort was re-constructed. As a result of ongoing archeological work at the fort, the stockade was dismantled in the early 1960s and re-built based on new evidence and information. Today the fort is open for visitors and hosts a variety of re-enactment events. Visitors are able to interact with archeologists who continue to investigate the history of the fort every summer. Together with Fort Mackinac and several related area locations,

Fort Michilimackinac is one of the must-visit locations in Michigan.

Here is the text of the Michigan state historical marker at the fort:

Around 1715 Constant Le Marchand de Lignery established Fort Michilimackinac for the French at the site of a Jesuit Mission. During the next fifty years as France and Great Britain struggled for control of the fur trade in the Great Lakes region, the fort expanded as a trading settlement and a military post. Soon after hostilities of the French & Indian War ceased, the British took control of the fort in the fall of 1761. Two years later local Chippewa (Ojibwa), angered by the British policies, captured the fort as part of Pontiac's Uprising. The British regained control in 1764. Between 1779 and 1781, during the American Revolution, the British built Fort Mackinac on nearby Mackinac Island and abandoned Fort Michilimackinac.

The British military abandoned and burned Fort Michilimackinac in 1781. Set aside as part of a village park in 1857, the fort site was placed under the direction of the Mackinac Island State Park Commission in 1909. In 1933 the fort's stockade was rebuilt after the park custodian unearthed the foundations of the palisade. Always popular, especially among campers, the park saw visitation boom after the Mackinac Bridge opened in 1957. In 1959 professional archaeologists began investigation the site. Their findings prompted the dismantling of the stockade and reconstruction of the fort based on archaeological evidence. The excavation of Fort Michilimackinac is one of the longest ongoing archaeological projects in North America.

Chapter 38

A depiction of the 1763 Siege of Fort Detroit by
artist Frederic Remington (U.S. Army)

Name: Fort Pontchartrain du Detroit or Fort Detroit
Location: Detroit (Wayne County)
Year Built: 1701
Disposition: Destroyed by Great Detroit Fire, June 11, 1805
Owner: France, 1701-Nov. 29, 1760; Britain, Nov. 29, 1760-1795; U.S., 1795-1805
Interesting fact: The founding of the fort in July 1701 is considered the birth of the city of Detroit.
Web site: http://historydetroit.com/places/fort_british.php

The establishment of Fort Pontchartrain du Detroit, later known simply as Fort Detroit, marks the birth date of Michigan's largest city–July 24, 1701. After having left his posting at Fort de Buade in St. Ignace (see page 76), as he sought a location where he could better prevent British fur traders from entering the region, Antoine de la Mothe Cadillac arrived on Grosse Ile in the Detroit River on July 23, 1701. The following day, he moved on to the mainland in what is now part of downtown Detroit. Construction began shortly thereafter on Fort Pontchartrain de troit--"on the straits."– The fort was named for the French official–Count Jerome de Pontchartrain--who authorized Cadillac to make the move from St. Ignace to Detroit. From his new outpost at Detroit, Cadillac claimed the surrounding territory in the name of France and sought to control the area fur trade.

Immediately after arriving in Detroit, Cadillac began the construction of the stockade fort. The first completed building of the project was the original Ste. Anne's Church, which was the first established European church in southeast Michigan and is believed to be the second-oldest Catholic parish in continual operation in the U.S. The walls of the stockade, made of logs and measuring some 12 feet high in the corner battlements, were completed shortly thereafter. The original fort was bordered by the modern-day streets of Griswold, Fort, Shelby and Larned. Cadillac would command the fort through 1712, when he was removed due to questions over his alleged corruption in overseeing trade with area Native Americans–the same allegations that had dogged him during his command in St. Ignace. For more on Cadillac, see page 234.

The fort was involved in various skirmishes between the French and various Native American tribes over the years. Most notable was the 1712 attack on Detroit, during which some 1,000 Fox, Sac and Mascouten warriors attacked the fort. The Fox had heard of Cadillac's removal as commander and decided to launch the attack during a perceived moment of weakness for the French. The French were severely outnumbered at the time, as their allies, the Ottawas and the Hurons, were away on a raid of their own at the time. As the attack was mounting, however, the French were able to slip a messenger out of the fort to bring the Ottawas and the Huronsback to the rescue. During the battle, a large group of Fox warriors were trapped on what is now Windmill Pointe in Grosse Pointe. The Fox warriors are said to have agreed to surrender and disarm, to spare their families, who were with them. After the warriors disarmed, they were attacked and killed by the French, Ottawas and Hurons. That event was considered the opening to the Fox Wars which continued through 1716 and flared up again in the 1720s and 1730s.

In the 1750s, the French officially changed the name of the fort from Fort Pontchartrain to Fort Detroit.

During the French & Indian War, 1754-1763, Fort Detroit served mainly as a supply center for warriors aligned with the French. The war Britain against France, with both countries largely fighting through their Native American allies as proxies. No major battles of that war were fought at the fort. The French & Indian War was a part of the larger, essentially worldwide Seven Years War, in which Britain scored a defeat of France. With that victory, Britain took possession of vast swaths of France's claims in the New World. Due to the distances involved, however, it would not be until Nov. 29, 1760, when a 30-man company of the British Army's Rogers Rangers took possession of Fort Detroit and began flying the British flag over the fort and therefore the southeast Michigan region for the first time.

With the departure of their French allies, Ottawa chief Pontiac staged an uprising against the British and attacked Fort Detroit on May 7, 1763. This action eventually came to be known as the Siege at Fort Detroit. The attack on Detroit was part of a larger series of actions across the Great Lakes region, centered in Michigan, known as Pontiac's Rebellion.

Unable to capture the fort in his initial attack, Pontiac and his warriors lay siege to the fort and its garrison of 130 British soldiers. The siege lasted for two months until a British force of 250 additional soldiers arrived on the scene and began to attack Pontiac's forces. The two sides battled throughout the summer and fall until Pontiac's forces were finally beaten back in mid-November 1763. For more on Chief Pontiac, see page 243.

During the Revolutionary War, just as during the French & •

Indian Wars, Detroit was too far remote to be a key factor in any battles. Just as the French had done, however, the British used the fort to supply and encourage Native American raids on Colonial interests. In response, an American force, led by George Rogers Clark, attacked the fort in Detroit. Too undermanned to win the battle, Clark's men did manage to capture the lieutenant-governor of Canada, Henry Hamilton, who was at the fort and hold him for a time as a prisoner of war. This was likely the key catalyst to cause British Capt. Richard Lernoult to begin construction of a new, stronger fort a few hundred yards to the south of the existing fort. This new fort was named Fort Lernoult (see page 91) upon its completion on Oct. 3, 1779. With its completion, the British moved the bulk of their military force to the new location.

Under the terms of the Jay Treaty, signed July 11, 1796, Fort Detroit, Fort Lernoult and the surrounding area was ceded by the British to the U.S. The original Fort Detroit was apparently completely destroyed in a major fire on June 11, 1805, that destroyed most of the Detroit community.

Here is the text from the state of Michigan historical marker for the original Fort Pontchartrain du Detroit as well as several other related nearby markers:

> *The first permanent French settlement in the Detroit region was built on this site in 1701. The location was recommended by Antoine de la Mothe Cadillac, who wished to move the fur trade center south from Fort de Buade. Cadillac's plan was approved by Count Jerome de Pontchartrain, Minister of Marine, for whom the fort was named. The term le detroit (the strait) was applied to the fort and surrounding area; after 1751 the post was known as Fort Detroit. In 1760, as a result of the French & Indian War, the British gained control of Detroit and other posts in the Great Lakes region. British troops enlarged Fort Detroit, but during the American Revolution they moved to nearby Fort Lernoult, built in 1778-79. The Americans occupied Fort Lernoult in 1796 and renamed it*

Fort Shelby.

Battle of Bloody Run, Detroit

Near this site, in late July 1763, the British and Indians fought the fiercest battle of Chief Pontiac's uprising. As Captain James Dalyell led about 260 soldiers across Parent's Creek, the Indians launched a surprise attack which devastated the British. Dalyell and some sixty of his men were killed, and the creek became known as Bloody Run. This battle marked the height of Pontiac's siege of Detroit, a struggle which he was forced to abandon three months later.

Landing of Cadillac, Detroit

After departing Montreal June 5, 1701 <u>Antoine de la Mothe Cadillac</u> and his convoy of seventy-five canoes sailed down this river and on the evening of July 23 camped sixteen miles below the present city of Detroit on what is now Grosse Ile. On the morning of July 24, Cadillac returned upriver and reached a spot on the shore near the present intersection of West Jefferson and Shelby. Pleased with the strategic features, the bank towering some thirty feet above the level of the river, Cadillac landed and planted the flag of France, taking posession of the territory in the name of King Louis XIV. The erection of a fortress was immediately begun. The stockade, formed of fifteen-foot oak pickets set three feet into the ground, occupied an area of about an acre. The fortress was named <u>Fort Pontchartrain du Detroit</u> (the strait) in honor of Count Jerome de Pontchartrain, Minister of Marine. From this fort and settlement, Detroit, the Renaissance City, takes its origin. (opposite side of above is in French)

Fox Indian Massacre, Grosse Pointe

Encouraged by a potential alliance with the English, the

Fox Indians besieged Fort Pontchartrain, Detroit, in 1712. Repulsed by the French and their Huron and Ottawa Indian allies, the Fox retreated and entrenched themselves in this area known as Presque Isle. The French pursued and defeated the Fox in the only battle fought in the Grosse Pointes. More than a thousand Fox Indians were killed in a fierce five-day struggle. Soon afterward French settlers began to develop the Grosse Pointes.

Chapter 39

Name: Fort Repentigny, or Fort Chevalier de Repentigny
Location: Sault Ste. Marie (Chippewa County)
Established: 1750
Disposition: Burned by Ojibwe tribe, 1762.
Owners: French, 1750-1760; British, 1760-1762

The first fort to be built in Sault Ste. Marie, Fort Chevalier de Repentigny, or shortened to Fort Repentigny, was established in 1750 (some histories suggest the fort was established in 1751). Markers in Brady Park in the city denote the former location of the fort. The fort was built by the French Capt. Louis le Gardeur de Repentigny, who would later go on to fight alongside the American colonists in the Revolutionary War, similar to his more famous countryman the Marquis de Lafayette. The fort was originally built to protect French interests in the area's fur trade. The fort featured a 110-square foot stockade that enclosed four wooden houses.

In 1760, during the French & Indian War, the British captured the fort and took possession of it. On Dec. 28, 1762 (some sources say Dec. 22), as a precursor to Pontiac's Rebellion, which began in earnest in the spring of 1763, Ojibwe warriors attacked the fort and burned it to the ground.

In 1822, the original Fort Brady (see page 68) was built on the location of Fort Repentigny.

Chapter 40

Woodcut image of Fort Saginaw.

Name: Fort Saginaw
Location: Saginaw (Saginaw County)
Established: 1822
Disposition: Abandoned, 1824
Owners: U.S.
Interesting fact: Closed due to malaria outbreak

Spelled on some documents as Saguina or Sagana, Fort Saginaw was established by the U.S. Army in 1822 as a means to monitor and control the actions of the local Ojibwe tribe. The fort, located at the modern-day intersection of Hamilton and Court streets on the west bank of the Saginaw River in Saginaw, was garrisoned by a unit of the Third U.S. Infantry, under the command of Major Daniel Baker. The fort consisted of a blockhouse surrounded by a stockade and included barracks and quarters for officers.

Mosquito infestation along the river caused an outbreak of malaria in 1824 and the fort was abandoned. The area around the fort was eventually developed into the city of Saginaw. The site of the former fort was occupied by the Fordney Hotel, which was destroyed in a massive fire in 1991.

Chapter 41

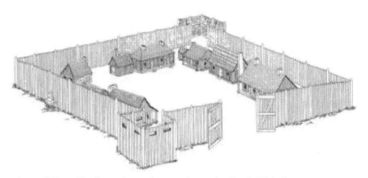

Drawing of Fort St. Joseph, as it may have looked. This image was created by Western Michigan University based on the long-ongoing archeology project at the fort. (Western Michigan University)

Name: Fort St. Joseph
Location: Niles (Berrien County)
Year Built: 1691
Disposition: Abandoned 1795. Site of an extensive archeological project administered by Western Michigan University.
Owner: France 1691-1761; Britain 1761-1763; Potawatomi tribe, 1763-1766?; Britain, 1766?-1781; Spain, 1781; Britain, 1781-1795
Interesting fact: One of two forts in Michigan named St. Joseph
Web site: www.wmich.edu/fortstjoseph,   www.fortstjoseph-museum.org

In use for more than 100 years, Fort St. Joseph in Niles has the unique distinction of being the only Michigan fort to have been operated under the flag of three different European nations–England, France and Spain–as well as one Native American tribe. This history lends itself to the Niles area being known as the Four Flags region, as the area has been governed at one point or another under the U.S., British, French and Spanish flags.

In the 1680s, King Louis XIV of France provided a land grant to Jesuit missionaries to operate in the area that is now Niles. The priests dubbed it the Mission de Saint-Joseph. In 1691, the French established a fortified trading post along the lower St. Joseph River, where two major Native American trails, the east-west Old Sauk Trail and the north-south Grand River Trail, met and cross the river. The French occupied the fort with a small garrison of soldiers for 70 years. Throughout that time, it served as a key hub of French commercial activity in the region.

In 1761, with the British victory in the French & Indian Wars, France turned over the Michigan territory to the British, causing control of Fort St. Joseph to change allegiances. The first British soldiers, a squad of about 15 troops, arrived in October 1761.

During a series of battles between several Native American tribes and the British known as Pontiac's Rebellion (see page 248), a group of Potawatomi warriors captured the fort on May 25, 1763, killing most of the garrison and taking the fort's commanding officer, Ensign Francis Schlosser, captive. Schlosser was later taken to Detroit, where he was ransomed back to the British Army. The Potawatomi maintained control over the fort area for the next several years.

By 1766, peace was brokered between the various warring factions of Pontiac's Rebellion. The new peace agreement allowed the British to eventually regain control of Fort St. Joseph. While troops were no longer stationed there on a regular basis, it did serve as an important trading hub for British concerns.

During the American Revolution, the British used Fort St. Joseph as a hub to provide weapons and other supplies to Native American tribes who allied with the British during the war against the American Colonies.

In 1781, a Spanish expedition, working in conjunction with Native American allies, traveled from St. Louis, Mo., to conduct a raid on the fort. The small Spanish force, under the command of Captain Don Eugenio Pouré, and its Native allies were able to win control of the fort. They flew the Spanish flag over the fort and spent a day looting it. The Spanish then returned to St. Louis, leaving the fort empty behind them. The attack by Spain was seen by many as a way for Spain to make territorial claims in the New World after a power vacuum was created following the British defeat in the War for Independence.

After a series of conflicts and battles across the country, the fledgling United States emerged victorious from the Northwest Indian War in 1795. In that same year, the U.S. and Britain signed Jay's Treaty and the U.S. and Spain signed Pinckney's Treaty, both of which eliminated any European claim over Michigan, though Britain regained control of Michigan during the War of 1812.

With the signing of the treaties, the British abandoned Fort St. Joseph in 1795. The fort eventually fell into disrepair and was "lost" to time. The exact location of the fort was rediscovered in 1998.

Today, the 15-acre site is home to a museum and other activities. Fort St. Joseph is also the site of an extensive, ongoing archeological project directed by Western Michigan University. Through WMU, various open houses and summer archeology camps are held at the site. See the web sites above for information on these activities.

The fort site is on both the state and national register of historic places. The state of Michigan historical marker at the fort reads:

> *"The French fort built here in 1691 controlled southern Michigan's principal Indian trade routes. Missionaries and fur traders were here already. The fort became a British outpost in 1761. Two years later it was one of the forts seized by Indians during the uprising of Chief Pontiac. Still later, traders made it their headquarters. In 1781 Spanish raiders ran up the flag of Spain at the fort for a few hours."*

Chapter 42

Name: Fort St. Joseph
Location: Port Huron (St. Clair County)
Year Built: 1686
Disposition: Abandoned and burned by own troops, 1688
Owner: France
Interesting fact: One of two forts named St. Joseph

Operated for just two years, this French fort in Port Huron was one of two to bear the name St. Joseph. In 1686, Daniel Greysolon, also known as Sieur du Lhut or DuLuth, established the fort, one of several in the Great Lakes region he established as a means to control the area's fur trade. Du Lhut would later become the name sake of the Lake Superior city of Duluth, Minn.

In 1687, a force of about 200 French trappers and traders, along with some 500 Native Americans of the Algonquin tribe, gathered at the fort to prepare for a major attack on the Six Nations Iroquois Confederacy. The attack-planning session evolved into a raucous drinking party that stretched on for several days and never led to any major battles.

In 1688, the fort's commander, Louis Armand de Lomd'Arce, also known as Baron de Lahontan, received news that French forces had abandoned the fort at Niagara. This news meant that a shipment of supplies for Fort St. Joseph would not arrive from Fort Niagara in New York as expected to help the 50 or so French soldiers at St. Joseph to make it through the winter. This news, plus increased Native American hostile activities in the area, prompted Lahontan to abandon and burn Fort St. Joseph and to take his troops, plus several dozen Native American allies, to Fort de Buade in St. Ignace (see page 76). More than 125 years later, the site 81), when that post was established in 1814.

There is a state of Michigan historical marker at the site of Fort St. Joseph and it reads:

Built near here in 1686 by the French explorer Duluth, this fort was the second white settlement in Lower Michigan. This post guarded the upper end of the vital waterway joining Lake Erie and Lake Huron. Designed to bar English traders from the upper lakes, the fort in 1687 was the mobilization center for a war party of French and Indians. In 1688 it was abandoned, but the site became part of Fort Gratiot in 1814.

Chapter 43

Name: Fort Sinclair or Fort St. Clair
Location: St. Clair (St. Clair County)
Established: 1764
Disposition: Abandoned 1785
Owner: British

Fort Sinclair, also known as Fort St. Clair, was built under the direction of Lt. Patrick Sinclair of the British Army in 1764 at the mouth of the Pine River, in the modern-day community of St. Clair. Over the next three years, Sinclair used the fort as a base of operations as he continued exploration and military patrols around the eastern Great Lakes, mostly operating from ships on the lakes. In 1767, his forces were reduced and he spent the next two years living full-time at the fort, before being recalled to England in 1769.

The fort continued to be garrisoned by a small detachment of soldiers, but was left empty several times during the 1770s. In 1785, it was abandoned for good and left to return to the elements.

Lt. Sinclair is most noted for his military leadership at Fort Mackinac (see page 100) in the late 1770s. For more on Patrick Sinclair, see page 244.

Chapter 44

Soldiers with the 1st Michigan Infantry line up at Fort Wayne in the 1860s, likely during the Civil War. (Detroit Public Library)

Montgomery Meigs (U.S. Army)

Name: Fort Wayne

Location: Detroit (Wayne County)

Established: 1842

Disposition: Transferred to city of Detroit, 1948-1976. Small portion of former fort property used by Army Corps of Engineers as boat yard.

Owners: U.S.

Interesting fact: Known as the fort to "never fire its guns in anger."

Web site: www.historicfortwaynecoalition.com

Fort Wayne was the third of three forts built in Detroit and the only one of the three to be built by the U.S. government. In 1841, Congress authorized a series of forts along the northern border, including one at Detroit. The previous forts in Detroit -- Fort Ponchartrain see page 111 and Fort Lernoult/Shelby (see page 91) -- had been abandoned and destroyed decades before and a fort was needed in Detroit to serve as a counterpoint to Fort Malden in Amherstburg, Ontario, Canada. The fort was named in honor of Revolutionary War general and hero "Mad" Anthony Wayne. For more on Anthony Wayne, see Page 245.

The history of the site where Fort Wayne stands today dates back to long before the first British colonists arrived in the New World. The location of the fort, 96 acres at the foot of Livernois Avenue, is along the shore of the Detroit River, at one of its narrowest points, about half a mile across. Ancient Native American burial mounds on the grounds of the fort are believed to date back to approximately 1000 A.D.

The military history of the land where the fort sits pre-dates the construction of the fort by a couple of decades. In the early 1800s, the fort's location was not yet included in the Detroit city limits and the area was part of Springwell Township. The location's relative proximity to Canada – across the river was the former Ontario city of Sandwich, which has since become part of Windsor – allowed militia troops to bombard the Canadians with cannon fire on July 4, 1812, which may have been the first shots fired in the War of 1812. Later, during that same war, British troops landed at "the sand hill at Springwells" and marched on to capture Fort Shelby, which was part of the city proper. In 1815, U.S. officials met with leaders of several area Native American tribes at the site of the future fort. There, the U.S. and the tribes signed the Treaty of Springwells, which officially ended hostilities between the U.S. and the various tribes that had sided with the British during the War of 1812. Among those representing the U.S. in that meeting was Lewis Cass, who would later serve as a territorial governor of Michigan and later as a U.S. senator after Michigan became a state. Also present that day was General William Henry Harrison, who would become the 9th U.S. president in 1845. For more on Lewis Cass, see page 235.

With the close of the War of 1812, the area that would eventually become Fort Wayne was peacefully used as farmland for a couple of decades before plans were laid for the creation of a new fort. Shortly after Congress laid out the plans for the string of forts along the northern border, Army Lt. Montgomery C. Meigs was sent to Detroit to build a fort. Meigs purchased farms along the river and began construction of the fort–about three miles down river from downtown Detroit–in 1842. Initial construction on all of the fort's primary structures was completed by 1851 at a cost of $150,000. (The Fort Meigs in Perrysburg, Ohio, which also played a pivotal role in the War of 1812, is named for Return J. Meigs, Jr., a cousin of Montgomery. Return Meigs served as Ohio governor during the War of 1812.)

For most of its roughly 120-year history as an active military fort, Fort Wayne was primarily a staging and processing center of sorts. During the Civil War, World War I and the conflicts in Korea and Vietnam, Fort Wayne was an induction and mustering center for troops being sent off to war. During World War II, the fort was used for those purposes, but was also a command and control center for the purchasing of automobiles and related parts and equipment for the Army's fleet of tanks, Jeeps and related vehicles.

By the time the initial construction of the fort was complete in

1851, the U.S. and Britain–and by extension, Canada–had resolved most of their outstanding differences and began friendships that, other than some tensions during the U.S. Civil War, have continued to this day. The peace between the U.S. and Britain/Canada also meant that there was no real need for a fort in Detroit. For much of the 10 years between the fort's completion and the start of the Civil War, the fort was garrisoned by a force of exactly one man–a single watchman who maintained the grounds of the brand new fort. During this time, the fort also apparently had an unofficial, but highly noble purpose: it was used, at least a few times, as a stop along the Underground Railroad, along which escaped slaves traveled to Canada and to freedom.

In 1861, with the commencement of the U.S. Civil War, concern arose over British sympathies with the Confederate states and the possibility of raids from Canada into the Union. Fort Wayne was garrisoned throughout the war, though no such British intervention ever materialized. Within a couple of weeks of the opening shots between the North and the South in 1861, the 1st Michigan Volunteer Infantry Regiment mustered into service at Fort Wayne on Sept. 16, 1861. The 1st Michigan is the unit which, upon arriving in Washington D.C. at a particularly bleak moment for the Union cause, prompted President Abraham Lincoln to famously proclaim, "Thank God for Michigan!" (see page 251.) Several other Michigan units either officially mustered in or at least passed through Fort Wayne en route to the front lines throughout the Civil War.

Following the Civil War and into the late 1920s, Fort Wayne remained an active military garrison. During the Indian Wars in the Western United States, various units would at times be rotated off of duty in the West and sent to Fort Wayne for garrison duty as a break from front-line duty. Units from Fort Wayne were also sent to Cuba during the Spanish-American War and to the Philippines during the Philippine Insurrection, both in the late 1800s.

As the Detroit area auto industry began to grow in the early 1900s, Fort Wayne began to serve as the coordination center for the purchase of automotive parts, supplies and vehicles for the military. This activity ramped up somewhat during what was then known as The Great War, today called World War I. During World War II, this activity reached its peak, with a workforce of 2,000 civilians at the fort coordinating the flow of Jeeps, tanks and the like from Detroit's "Arsenal of Democracy" to the battlefields of Europe. Special railroad spurs were built on the fort property and a shipping dock was constructed on the riverfront to support this effort. Workers from the fort also set up a detachment at the Michigan State Fairground on the other side of Detroit to accommodate the flow of materials. Also during World War II, a significant number of Italian Prisoners of War were interned at the Fort.

Following World War I, America had its first "Red Scare" in roughly 1919-1921–a period of great worry and concern over the influence of communism. A number of alleged communists and suspected sympathizers were temporarily held in the stockade at Fort Wayne as they awaited trials. During the Great Depression, the Fort was the site of a major Civilian Conservation Corps camp, housing and employing hundreds of out-of-work men.

The size of the garrison at Fort Wayne was significantly reduced during the 1930s. Most of the activity at the fort during World War II was to support the motor vehicle manufacturing work being done in the region, with relatively few uniformed soldiers assigned to the fort. With victory in World War II, movements began to close the fort, which by now was passing the century mark of active duty. In 1948, the first transfer of the fort's property to the City of Detroit took place. The fort's original star-shaped fort and the original 1848 barracks, were transferred to the city's Historical Commission in 1948. The majority of the fort's property would be transferred to the city in various bits and pieces over the next 30 years.

Even as part of the fort began to be turned over to the city for use as a museum, the fort's service to the nation continued. During both the Korean and Vietnam conflicts, thousands of new soldiers, sailors, airmen and Marines were given physicals, sworn in and shipped out to basic training and other destinations. In the 1950s and into the 1960s, with America caught in the grip of the Cold War, anti-aircraft guns and, later, Nike and Ajax air-to-ground missiles were installed at the fort to defend the industrial might of Detroit against a feared bombing attack.

Some of the fort's vacant housing, no longer used by soldiers, were also pressed into service in 1967, following that summer's riots in Detroit when some displaced Detroiters were given temporary housing there. Some of those displaced by the riots stayed at the fort for more than two years.

Finally, in 1976, the last parcel of the fort was turned over to the city of Detroit, although the Army's Corps of Engineers retained control of about nine acres, which is now used as a boat yard. From the 1970s through the mid-2000s, the fort's land was controlled by the city's Historical Commission, with varying levels of activity as a museum and historic venue. Since 2006, the fort has been controlled by the city's recreation department, with extensive contributions by various nonprofit groups. The fort was used extensively as a venue during Detroit's 300th birthday celebration in 2001. Today, the fort's property continues to be used by various reenactment groups and as an educational historic site.

Numerous structures continue to exist at the fort, including the original barracks, which were built in 1848 and enhanced during the Civil War. A number of officer's homes, gun emplacements and other structures have been restored and maintained, though a number of buildings on the grounds are in advanced stages of decay.

Despite the fort's extensive 125-plus year history, it maintained an unexpected record: no gun at the fort was ever fired "in anger." In an interesting wrinkle of history, none of the historic cannons on display at the fort are pointed toward the Detroit River, as the fort's original use called for. The Treaty of Ghent, which ended the War of 1812, has specific guidelines which limit military operations around the Great Lakes and specifically prevent the U.S. from pointing large caliber weapons at Canada along the Great Lakes. This limitation has been interpreted to include historic weapons, such as 19th century cannons. As recently as the late 2000s, the Treaty of Ghent was revisited by the U.S. and Canada, to allow the Coast Guards of the two nations to upgrade the caliber of weapons used on their respective ships as they perform their law enforcement functions on the lakes.

Fort Wayne is on both the state and national list of historic locations. The Michigan Historic Marker at the fort reads:

> *No hostile shots have ever been fired from this star-shaped fort built in the 1840s to guard against a British invasion from Canada which never came. This third bastion to protect the river approach to the city was named for General "Mad" Anthony Wayne who accepted the surrender of Detroit from the British in 1796. It was a mobilization center for Union troops during the Civil War. Regiments from Fort Wayne served in the Indian conflicts, the Spanish-American War, the Philippine Insurrection, and World War I. An active post in the 1920s, it housed a Civilian Conservation Corps during the Depression. Fort Wayne was a wartime supply depot in World War II and an induction center during the Korean and Vietnam conflicts. Deactivated by the federal government in 1967, it now operates as a military museum under the auspices of the Detroit Historical Commission.*

Chapter 45

The officer quarters at Fort Wilkins as they appear today.
(State of Michigan)

Williams Wilkins (U.S. Army)

Name: Fort Wilkins
Location: Copper Harbor (Keweenaw County)
Established: 1844
Disposition: Deactivated, 1849; Re-activated, 1867; Abandoned, 1870. Currently a Michigan State Park.
Owner: U.S.
Interesting fact: Re-enactors simulate camp life at Fort Wilkins throughout the summer months.

Rivaling Fort Mackinac, if any place in Michigan can, as a must-visit location among Michigan's historic forts and related facilities, Fort Wilkins's remote solitude even today speaks of what life as a solder at the fort most have been like. In the summer months, re-enactors create an image of that life at this post at the extreme northern tip of the Keweenaw Peninsula. More than a dozen of the fort's building have either been restored or re-constructed and are open to visitors. Camping is available at the state park as well. One of the first lighthouses constructed on Lake Superior is also on the grounds of the park.

The fort was constructed by two companies of the 5th U.S. Infantry in 1844, under the command of General Hugh Brady (see page 231). The fort, named after Secretary of War William Wilkins, was constructed to provide protection and security for the growing copper mining industry in the region.

The fort's original stockade only covered two sides of the central compound of the fort, with Lake Fannie Hooe and a creek providing natural protections on the other two sides. The quarters for married enlisted men existed outside of the stockade.

The fort had only been garrisoned for two years when the Army left the fort empty as a result of a re-distribution of forces due to the Mexican-American War. The garrison left Fort Wilkins on July 24, 1846, leaving behind one man, Sgt. William Wright, to care for the camp. Wright died in 1855 and the fort was temporarily rented by a local doctor, who sought to turn the fort into a health resort. That plan ended with the death of the doctor in 1861. The post remained empty until it was reactivated in 1867, about two years after the conclusion of the U.S. Civil War. Three years later, the post was once again abandoned, this time for good, with the last troops leaving on Aug. 30, 1870.

In 1923, the state acquired the property, which had been privately held prior to that time, and turned the fort into a state park. During the Great Depression, the Works Projects Administration moved into the camp and restored and re-constructed the fort's buildings, turning it into one of the true jewels of the Michigan State Park system.

Here is the text of the Michigan state historical marker at Fort Wilkins:

As soon as miners began to enter the Copper Country, appeals were made to the army for protection from resentful Indians. Thus, in 1844, Fort Wilkins was built. Two companies of infantry stood guard at this early copper mining and shipping center. In 1846, during the Mexican War, the force was withdrawn. It was replaced only from 1867 to 1869.

Chapter 46

Emblem of the 906th Aircraft
Control and Warning Squadron.

Name: Grand Marais Air Force Station
Location: Grand Marais (Alger County)
Established: 1954
Disposition: Closed 1957. Abandoned.
Owners: U.S.
Interesting fact: One of several radar facilities across the state during the Cold War era.

Operating less than three full years, Grand Marais Air Force Station was located along Lake Superior in the Central Upper Peninsula. It was one of several Air Force radar stations opened in Michigan in the 1950s. During its brief operation, the site was manned by the 906th Aircraft Control and Warning Squadron.

The site was closed in 1957 in a budget cutting move. The property was then used as a private residence and later as the site of a saw mill. As of 2013, it is vacant, with some badly deteriorating buildings still standing.

Chapter 47

Name: Grosse Ile Stockade
Location: Grosse Ile (Wayne County)
Established: 1815
Disposition: Abandoned, 1819
Owners: U.S.

The Grosse Ile Stockade was built in 1815 to fend off concerns of a possible attack from British soldiers in Amhertsburg, Ontario, across the Detroit River. It was garrisoned by a detachment of the 5th Infantry Regiment and featured seven log cabins for barracks and a wooden fence. The stockade was abandoned in 1819. It was then used as a private home by the John Rucker family until 1835. The Stockade was located on East River Road on the east side of the island.

Here is the text of a Michigan historical marker East River Road on the island:

Military outpost

> *This point marked the northeast corner of the stockade of a post that was maintained on Grosse Ile by the United States Army for a short time after the War of 1812. The post was garrisoned by detachments of the Fifth Infantry Regiment which were quartered in seven log cabins. The troops protected the island's civilian population and their property from Indian raids.*

Chapter 48

Kincheloe Air Force Base, as it appeared from the air in 2006. (U.S. Geological Survey)

Capt. Iven C. Kincheloe
(U.S. Air Force)

Name: Kincheloe Air Force Base / Kinross Air Force Base / Kinross Auxiliary Airfield
Location: Kinross (Chippewa County)
Established: 1943
Disposition: Closed 1977. Used as an airport.
Owner: U.S.
Interesting fact: Was the site of the "Kinross Incident" an alleged UFO encounter.

One of the shortest lived major military installations of the modern era–in any state--Kinross Field: Kincheloe Air Force Base was one of three Cold War era Strategic Air Command bases in Michigan that were equipped with nuclear bomb-capability for the B-52 Stratofortress bombers.

Located about halfway between Sault Ste. Marie and St. Ignace in the Eastern Upper Peninsula, the field, in Chippewa County's Kinross Township, was opened as Kinross Auxiliary Airfield in 1943 with three 5,520-foot runways arranged in a triangle pattern. The field was originally a sub-base of Alpena Army Airfield (see page 16). Initially, no aircraft were assigned to the base and it was used as a refueling stop and as a staging area, if needed, for defense of the locks in the St. Mary's River at Sault Ste. Marie.

After the U.S. victory in World War II, the base was inactivated and was leased to the city of Sault Ste. Marie for use as an airport. On July 1, 1952, the field was reactivated as Kinross Air Force Base as an Air Defense Command base. The 4685th Air Base Squadron, later designated as the 91st Air Base Squadron, was the first command element at the base. The runways at the base were extended and the facility was built up to accommodate assigned aircraft for the first time. On Feb. 16, 1953, the 534th Group was stood up at Kinross, flying the F-94 Starfire and later the F-89 Scorpion.

It was on Nov. 23, 1953, that the most famous–or infamous– event in Kinross AFB history took place. Known as the "Kinross Incident," an F-89 was scrambled from the base that night, assigned to find and identify, a "radar blip"–a report of an unidentified object in the sky. The aircraft and crew, pilot Lt. Felix Eugene Moncla, Jr., and radar operator Lt. Robert L. Wilson, apparently vanished during the mission. Neither man nor the aircraft have apparently ever been recovered, as of 2013. Various theories as to the fate of Lt. Moncla and his aircraft have arisen over the years, including that the radar blip was that of a way-ward cargo aircraft flown by the Royal Canadian Air Force, though Canada officially denied that they had an aircraft in the area at a time. The official Air Force accident report suggests a crash into Lake Superior, causing the aircraft to break apart on impact. UFO theorists have long suggested that another flying object–origins unknown–was involved in the loss of the plane and the airmen.

In September 1959, Kinross AFB was renamed Kincheloe Air Force Base in honor of America's "First Spaceman," Iven C. Kincheloe. Air Force Capt. Kincheloe, a native of Cassopolis, Mich., had, in 1956, become the first pilot of any nation to fly above 100,000 feet when the X-2 rocket-powered aircraft he was flying hit an altitude of 126,200 feet. In July 1958, Kincheloe was killed in the crash of an F-104 Starfighter that he was piloting, in a test flight at Edwards AFB in California. Kincheloe was also an Air Force ace, having recorded five aerial victories during the Korean War.

In 1962, Kincheloe AFB came under the authority of the Strategic Air Command. The 449th Bomb Wing was assigned to the base, along with a fleet of B-52 aircraft. Shortly thereafter, a plan was announced to close the base at the end of that decade. Political wrangling killed that plan, but the base was again targeted for closure during the 1970s. The base was inactivated in 1977.

The former base is now the site of Chippewa County International Airport, a major state prison and a small community known as Kincheloe, using the former military housing at the base area.

Chapter 49

Name: K.I. Sawyer Air Force Base
Location: Gwinn (Marquette County)
Established: 1955
Disposition: Closed 1995. Used as an airport
Owners: U.S.
Interesting fact: One of the very few military bases in the U.S. that was not named for a military hero or battle.

In the 1930s, Marquette County Road Commissioner Kenneth I. Sawyer began advocating a plan for a regional airport in that central Upper Peninsula county. An initial airport was developed near Negaunee. When that airport proved inadequate to accommodate the growing local interest in aviation, a second airport was developed near the small town of Gwinn. In the opening year of World War II, a plan was floated to designate the new airport as a military airfield, but the plan was rejected by the Army. In 1944, Sawyer died and the airport was named in his honor.

With the expansion of the U.S. Air Force's national footprint in the 1950s in response to the Cold War, the Sawyer airport got another look. On Jan. 24, 1955, the Air Force signed a 99-year lease on the airport and for a couple of years, the base operated as a joint civilian-military air field. On May 8, 1959, the field became a strictly military operation and was officially dubbed K.I. Sawyer Air Force Base.

The base started as part of Air Defense Command and the first aircraft at the base were F-102 Delta Daggers assigned to the 484th Fighter Interceptor Squadron of the 473rd Fighter Group at the base. In 1959, the runway was expanded to 12,300 feet long and the 56th Fighter Wing became the host unit at the base, flying F-101 Voodoos and later F-106 Delta Darts.

On Jan. 1, 1964, K.I. Sawyer was transferred to the Strategic Air Command and the 410th Bomb Wing became the host unit on the base. With the movement, B-52 Stratofortresses and KC-135

Stratotankers became the primary aircraft assigned to the base.

In 1993, the decision was made by the Air Force to close Sawyer, along with a number of other bases, as part of the draw down following the end of the Cold War. The base's last B-52 left in November 1994. The base was officially closed on Sept. 30, 1995. Since the closure, a portion of the base has been used as Sawyer International Airport. Other parts of the base were sold to private interests for a variety of residential and commercial uses. The K.I. Sawyer Heritage Museum is also open on the former base, featuring six different aircraft that were used at the base over the years, including a B-52.

Chapter 50

Naval Air Station Grosse Ile as it looked in 1947. (U.S. Navy)

President George H.W.
Bush (White House)

Name: Naval Air Station Grosse Ile (also, OLF Newport)
Location: Grosse Ile (Wayne County)
Established: 1929

Disposition: Closed 1969. Some of former base used for township municipal offices.

Owners: U.S.

Interesting fact: U.S. President George H.W. Bush was among the thousands of Navy pilots trained at the island base.

A key training site for Navy pilots during World War II, Naval Station Grosse Ile had a storied 50-plus year history in the middle of the 20th Century. The legacy of the air station is maintained today with many of its facilities still in use as an active general aviation airport. A small museum is on the property as well, preserving the history of the air station.

Though it was officially commissioned as a Naval Reserve Base on Sept. 7, 1929, Grosse Ile history with the Navy actually goes back to July 1925, when four Navy reservists started a unit there. Operating without a single aircraft for over a year, the reservists busied themselves with classroom instruction. Eventually, the Navy sent an NY-1 seaplane to the station for training use. The base's first structure was a large tin hangar built in Detroit and then floated down the Detroit River to the island. At the time the Navy was beginning to operate at Grosse Ile, the Detroit Aircraft Corp. also had operations there and the Curtiss Company, later the Curtiss-Wright Company, operated a flying school at the field. By 1935, the land formerly utilized by those operations had been acquired by the Navy and the base was taking shape.

In the middle-late 1920s, the ZMC-2, an all-metal airship–it looked like a dirigible but with a metal skin–was built by the Detroit Aircraft Corp. at the site and was acquired by the Navy. The so-called "Tin Blimp" first took flight at Grosse Ile, but was assigned to duty at a base in New Jersey upon completion.

With the onset of World War II, the base was officially re-christened as Naval Air Station Grosse Ile. During the war, more than 5,000 Navy pilots and more than 1,000 British Royal Air Force pilots received initial flight training at the base. Among those trained there were future President George H.W. Bush and game show host Bob Barker. A wide variety of aircraft was assigned to the base during the war years. During the war, the station achieved its maximum size: about 604 acres.

Following World War II, the base was used for a variety of functions and was home for many years to a squadron of A-1 Skyraiders; an anti-submarine warfare unit; and various Navy and Marine Corps reserve units. Also, during the Cold War, a Nike-Ajax missile site was on the base, operated by the U.S. Army.

In 1969, the Navy closed the Grosse Ile station and relocated Naval air operations to Selfridge Air Force Base (now Selfridge Air National Guard Base) (see page 168) on the opposite side of the Detroit metro region.

The station's former Hangar 1 is now the Grosse Ile Township Office.

The Navy also operated 16 "outlying fields"--or OLFs--from Grosse Ile. These facilities were generally mostly civilian or barren air strips that Navy trainees could use for landings and take offs. All of the OLFs were located in southern Wayne County or in Monroe County. OLF Newport was the most extensive of these operations was later used as a Nike Missile site during the Cold War era. The Navy also built several buildings at Newport to support operations there. Some of the Navy-constructed buildings at the OLF were later used as a high school building. Newport was also used to house German Prisoners of War for almost two years at the end and just after World War II. Some of the up to 18 buildings built by the Navy at Newport are still standing. With the exception of Newport, all of the OLFs were only operated for the duration of the war and ceased being used for military functions shortly thereafter. The OLFs in Michigan, all of which supported NAS Grosse Ile, were:

Ash Field
Bolles Harbor Field
Blackmore Field
Brownstown Field
Custer Field
Dauncy Field

Flat Rock Field
Leathers Field
Maybee Field
Masserant Field
Monroe Field
Navarre Field
Newport Field
Sanders Field
Scofield Field
Sheep Ranch Field

Some of the OLFs were known by different names at various times. The names above were taken from a 1942 map created by the Navy.

Chapter 51

The Polar Bear Monument at the
White Chapel Cemetery in Troy.

Name: Polar Bear Monument
Location: Troy (Oakland County)
Established: 1930
Disposition: Still in existence
Owners: U.S.
Interesting fact: Honors World War I era unit known as "Detroit's Own"

Though not a military installation, the Polar Bear monument at the White Chapel Cemetery in Troy is a testament to a now mostly-forgotten group of Michigan soldiers who suffered significant hardship in service to their nation. The Detroit's Own regiment were sent to remote northern Russia during the Russian Revolution as an attempt by the U.S. to encourage Russia to participate in World War I. The plight of the unit was mostly-overshadowed by the larger events of World War I. The unit had originally trained and been organized at Michigan's Fort Custer (see page 73).

Here is the text of the Michigan state historical marker at the monument, which was erected at the cemetery, burial place for a number of the unit's soldiers, in 1930.

Polar Bears, Troy

In the summer of 1918, President Woodrow Wilson, at the urging of Britain and France, sent an infantry regiment to north Russia to fight the Bolsheviks in hopes of persuading Russia to rejoin the war against Germany. The 339th Infantry Regiment with the first battalion of the 310th Engineers and the 337th Ambulance and Hospital Companies, arrived at Archangel, Russia on September 4, 1918. About 75 percent of the 5,500 Americans who made up the North Russian Expeditionary Forces were from Michigan; of those, a majority were from Detroit. The newspapers called them "Detroit's Own,"; they called themselves "Polar Bears." They marched on Belle Isle on July 4, 1919. Ninety-four of them were killed in action after the United States decided to withdraw from Russia but before Archangel's harbor thawed.

In 1929 five former "Polar Bears" of the 339th Infantry Regiment returned to north Russia in an attempt to recover the bodies of fellow soldiers who had been killed in action or died of exposure ten years earlier. The group was selected by members of the Polar Bear Association under the auspices of the Veterans of Foreign Wars. The trip was sponsored by the federal government and the State of Michigan. The delegates recovered eight-six bodies. Fifty-six of these were buried on this site on May 30, 1930. The Polar Bear Monument was carved from white Georgia marble; the steps from black North Carolina granite. The black granite base symbolizes a fortress, and the cross and helmet denote war burial.

Chapter 52

Emblem of the 754th Aircraft Control
And Warning (later, Radar) Squadron.

Name: Port Austin Air Force Station
Location: Port Austin (Huron County)
Established: 1951
Disposition: Closed 1988. Buildings used for a variety of purposes, some abandoned.
Owners: U.S.
Interesting fact: One of several radar facilities across the state during the Cold War era.

Port Austin Air Force Station was among a half-dozen or so Air Force radar installations in Michigan that operated as part of the Air Defense Command system during the Cold War. The 754th Aircraft Control and Warning (later, Radar) Squadron began operating the station in July 1951. It was closed in late 1988. The station is located in the village of Port Austin, at the tip of Michigan's Thumb.

Many of the station's buildings still exist and many of them have been converted into a variety of uses, some private and some used by local government.

Along with the Calumet Air Force Station, Port Austin was the last of the operational Air Force stations in Michigan.

Chapter 53

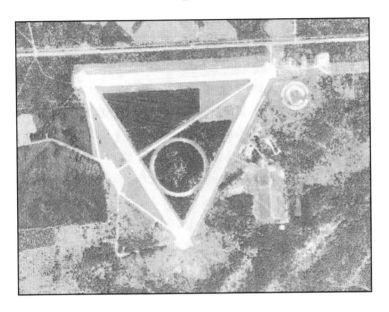

Raco Army Airfield as it appeared in 2000. (U.S. Geological Survey)

Name: Raco Army Airfield (later, Raco Auxiliary Airfield)
Location: 24 miles west/southwest of Sault Ste. Marie (Chippewa County)
Established: 1940
Disposition: Closed 1972. Now known as the Smithers Winter Test Center, privately-owned center used for testing automobiles in extreme weather conditions.
Owners: U.S.
Interesting fact: Now a cold weather test facility

The rural Raco Army Airfield was created in 1940, shortly before the U.S. entered World War II in late 1941. After the U.S. entered the war, the base was expanded and three runways, in a triangle formation, were built. During the war, the base was minimally staffed and was under the command of the 4250th Army Air Force Base Unit at the air field in Alpena. During the war, a small contingent of U.S. Navy personnel was also briefly assigned to the base. Sometime shortly after the U.S. entry into the war, the base was re-named Raco Auxiliary Airfield.

Following the war, as the U.S. entered the Cold War era, the air field was used as an anti-aircraft artillery site, with several artillery units scattered around the base. The artillery was intended to protect the important Sault Ste. Marie locks and shipping channel from attack, as well as provide protection for the industrial centers in southeast Michigan. By 1956, the development and deployment of the Nike/Ajax missile systems, as well as the presence of jet-powered fighter-interceptor aircraft at K.I. Sawyer Air Force Base (see page 142) near Marquette, rendered the artillery at Raco obsolete.

In 1960, the base briefly took on a new life when the 27th Air Defense Missile Squadron was stood up on the base and equipped with long range "BOMARC" surface-to-air missiles. At that time, the missile's command center became known as the Kincheloe AFB BOMARC site. Even with this activity, fewer than 100 military personnel were assigned to the base.

In 1972, the missile operation was inactivated and the property was sold to private owners. The site remains in private hands and is now used as a cold weather test site, primarily serving the auto and truck industry.

Chapter 54

Name: River Raisin National Battlefield Park
Location: Monroe (Monroe County)
Established: 1813
Disposition: Opened as National Park in 2010
Owners: U.S.
Interesting fact: Site of the deadliest battle in Michigan history.

Though it commemorates an event that took place more than 200 years ago, the River Raisin National Battlefield Park is the new kid on the block in terms of visitor-friendly military locations in Michigan. For several decades the site of the actual Battle of the River Raisin in modern-day Monroe was occupied by a large paper mill. After many years of the paper mill sitting vacant, efforts by the city of Monroe and numerous other organizations and volunteers paved the way for a new park to be developed to mark the battle's site. In 2009, Congress passed legislation to make the battlefield a new National Battlefield Park. In 2010, the National Park Service took possession of 30 acres to create the park. A visitor's center is also available. Plans are in place to expand the park in the future.

The Battle of the River Raisin, also known as the River Raisin Massacre or the Battle of Frenchtown–as Monroe was known at the time–was by far the most deadly military battle in Michigan history and was also one of the largest land engagements of the War of 1812 anywhere in North America. The battle is typically considered to have been two separate, related events that took place several days apart, January 18-23, 1813. The battles at the River Raisin may represent the last, lowest point of American military operations on the North American continent, at least in terms of action against a foreign power. (In the terrible fighting of the Civil War, one must consider that an American army–be it Union or Confederate–was the victor in every battle.)

In the second half of 1812, Frenchtown was held by the British, as was the larger fort at Detroit (Detroit had been captured by the British in August 1812). When American Gen. William Hull surrendered Fort Detroit (see page 240), the community of Frenchtown was included in the terms of surrender. Frenchtown was shortly thereafter garrisoned by a small force of Canadian militiamen, bolstered by some area Native American allies. (Canada was still a part of the British Empire.) The Americans sought to change that situation and desired to march on Detroit from camps in Ohio. Frenchtown was to be the first stop on the way back to Detroit.

On Jan. 18, a force of more than 600 American soldiers under the command of Cols. William Lewis and John Allen arrived in Frenchtown, quickly overrunning the 63 Canadian militia and their approximately 200 Native American allies. The Americans quickly moved to strengthen their position, setting up defensive positions on the northern side of the river in Frenchtown. As they began to dig in, the Americans were re-enforced by about 400 or so troops under the command of American Gen. James Winchester, who now assumed control of the more than 1,000 Americans assembled at Frenchtown. The Americans assumed a defensive posture, awaiting the arrival of Gen. (and future president) William Henry Harrison for the eventual march and attack on Fort Detroit.

Before Harrison arrived, the British counterattack came. Moving across the ice of the frozen Lake Erie from their camp at Fort Malden in Amherstberg, Ontario, Canada, about 600 British and Canadian troops, along with some 800 Native Americans, led by warrior chief Tecumseh, attacked Frenchtown before dawn on Jan. 22, 1813, catching the Americans asleep. In less than 20 minutes, the 17th U.S. Infantry was routed and was in full, unorganized retreat across the frozen River Raisin and headed toward Ohio. Of the more than 400 Americans from the 17th, which had held the Americans' right flank, about 220 were killed and 147 were captured, including Gen. Winchester. Some 500 American militia men continued to hold behind the picket fence of Frenchtown until they were surprised by the official word–the captured Winchester had surrendered the town.

Despite their victory, the British forces were badly wounded and, fearing the eventual arrival of Harrison, removed from Frenchtown, leaving only a token guard force–and scores, perhaps hundreds of wounded American soldiers--behind. Into the vacuum that was created after the battle and reduction of forces, a group of Native American warriors moved into Frenchtown on Jan. 23, killing and/or capturing a number of Americans–estimates ranged from a half dozen to three dozen victims.

Upon hearing the news of the defeat at Frenchtown, Harrison declared the defeat a "national calamity." The nation as a whole responded by creating a new battle cry for the remainder of the War of 1812–"Remember the Raisin!"

Frenchtown was liberated by American forces in September 1813, a few days before Fort Detroit was re-taken by the Americans, as the British retreated to the north following a devastating defeat in the Battle of Lake Erie (Sept. 10, 1813) that essentially paved the way for the ultimate American victory in the War of 1812.

Two Michigan state historical markers in Monroe help tell some of the story of the River Raisin battles:

Michigan, Historic Crossroads

Because of its location in the heart of the upper Great Lakes, Michigan has been a historic crossroads. Its waterways and trails were favorite routes of Indians many centuries ago. French explorers first entered Michigan about 1620. By 1700 forts at several key points guarded this vital link between French colonies to the east and to the west and south. In 1760-1761 the British won control of Michigan. Not until 1796 did they withdraw in favor of the Americans, who had been awarded the area in 1783 at the end of the Revolutionary War. During the War of 1812, Michigan was one of the most fiercely contested areas. It was admitted as a state in 1837.

Monroe

Monroe, founded about 1784, is one of Michigan's oldest set-tlements. It was called Frenchtown after its original settlers. It was the site of the River Raisin Massacre during the War of 1812. Renamed Monroe in 1824, it later anchored the Michi-gan Southern Railroad and became famous for its paper and glass. General George Custer made his home here.

Chapter 55

Pilots of the Women Airforce Service Pilots, or WASP, program meet with an instructor pilot at Romulus Army Air Field.

Name: Romulus Army Air Field, also known as Romulus Field

Location: Romulus (Wayne County)

Year Built: 1929 (as Wayne County Airport)

Disposition: Greatly expanded and in civilian use at Detroit Metropolitan Airport

Owner: U.S.

Interesting fact: Was a key training site for the Women Airforce Service Pilots, or WASPs

Known today at Detroit Metropolitan Airport or simply as "Metro," Michigan's largest airport was used by various military organizations for parts of five decades. Planning for the airport was begun in 1927 and construction of the original airport was completed in late 1929. The first landing at the facility then called the Wayne County Airport, was on Feb. 22, 1930. The Michigan National Guard's 107th Observation Squadron began some level of activity at the new airport possibly as early as 1929 and was certainly in place by 1931.

During World War II, the facility was renamed Romulus Army Air Field. During the war, the Third Ferry Group, an organization of the Women Airforce Service Pilots, operated at the field, training hundreds of women for a variety of duties, including flying aircraft from the U.S. to Europe. It would not be until the 1970s that these women would be fully accorded "veteran" status for their service in World War II.

Following the conclusion of the war, the newly-created Michigan Air National Guard continued to operate at the airport until 1971 when the ANG relocated to Selfridge Air National Guard Base (see page 168).

Chapter 56

Emblem of the 753rd Aircraft Control and Warning Squadron.

Name: Sault Sainte Marie Air Force Station
Location: Sault Ste. Marie (Chippewa County)
Established: 1950/1952
Disposition: Closed 1979. Property and buildings used for a variety of private uses, primarily housing.
Owner: U.S.
Interesting fact: One of several radar facilities across the state during the Cold War era.

The 753rd Aircraft Control and Warning Squadron (later Radar Squadron) began operations in November 1950 at the Sault Ste. Marie Airport. On Jan. 1, 1952, the squadron moved to the newly-built Sault AFS to begin permanent operations. Later, the station became part of the Sault Ste. Marie Air Defense Sector, though the sector's headquarters were actually at K.I. Sawyer Air Force Base in Gwinn, near Marquette, not in the Soo. The sector command, which had control over all the radar stations in the Upper Peninsula and Wisconsin, was stood up in 1958 and was disbanded in 1966.

The station was closed in 1978 and most of its radar equipment was moved to an Air Force Station in upstate New York. Today, the site is used mostly for private housing, with some private business operating part of the former station. Many of the original buildings still stand.

Chapter 57

Former Detroit Lighthouse Depot building. (U.S. Coast Guard)

Canadian coast guard icebreaker Griffon and U.S. Coast Guard Cutter Bristol Bay work to flush an ice jam in the St. Clair River as part of Operation Coal Shovel during the 2009-2010 Great Lakes ice breaking season. (U.S. Coast Guard)

Name: Sector Detroit (and Detroit Lighthouse Depot)
Location: Detroit (Wayne County)
Established: 1876
Disposition: Still in operation
Owners: U.S.
Interesting fact: In third century of operations in same location.
Web site: http://www.uscg.mil/d9/sectdetroit/default.asp

Home to a Coast Guard cutter, several smaller vessels and a variety of regional offices, Coast Guard Sector Detroit has operated at the foot of Mount Elliott Avenue on the shore of the Detroit River since 1876. Sector Detroit is the home port of the 140-foot icebreaking tug USCGC Bristol Bay and is the headquarters for a number of subordinate commands located at the Sector office or at one of six small boat stations in Michigan and two small boat stations in Ohio. Coast Guardsmen and women assigned or supervised by Sector Detroit are involved in essentially every major Coast Guard mission, ranging from search and rescue to law enforcement, homeland security to ice breaking.

In continuous operation since 1876, the facility has undergone three major construction phases: the initial building in 1876, construction of the pier and buildings in 1918-22 and a major overhaul and renovation in 1988.

The Bristol Bay is the largest cutter assigned to Detroit. The cutter was built in 1978 and commissioned into service in Detroit in 1979. The ship is capable of breaking through up to three feet of ice. In addition to the cutter itself, the Bristol Bay often works with a special 120-foot barge designed to facilitate working on buoys and other aids to navigation in the Detroit River and surrounding waters.

Two other Bay-class cutters, the Katmai Bay in Sault Ste. Marie and the Biscayne Bay in St. Ignace, are also assigned to Michigan stations.

The former Detroit Lighthouse Depot is located across the

street from the Sector Detroit facility. Constructed in 1871-74, the depot was the central supply and administration center for all lighthouses in the Great Lakes. The site of the depot was previously used as a United States Marine Hospital, serving military personnel. The magnificent red brick, 3-story Lighthouse Depot building was vacated by the Coast Guard in the early 1990s and was sold to the city of Detroit. It has been minimally used for some city offices since that time.

Chapter 58

Station Grand Haven (U.S. Coast Guard)

U.S. Coast Guard Cutter Escanaba seen in 1935. The ship was home-ported in Grand Haven for about 10 years. It was sunk by enemy action during World War II. (U.S. Coast Guard)

Name: Sector Field Office Grand Haven / Station Grand Haven

Location: Grand Haven (Ottawa County)
Established: 1875
Disposition: Still in use
Owner: U.S.
Interesting fact: Grand Haven is known as Coast Guard City, U.S.A.

Should for any reason, the U.S. Coast Guard ever need to move its national headquarters out of Washington, D.C. to a new location, Grand Haven would likely be at the head of the list. By an official act of Congress in 1998, Grand Haven was designated Coast Guard City, USA, recognizing the long, positive relationship between the city and the Coast Guard.

The first life saving station opened in Grand Haven in 1875 and the Coast Guard has had a presence there ever since. Today, Grand Haven serves as a station location and is also a sector field office for the Lake Michigan Sector, which is headquartered in Milwaukee on the opposite side of the lake. The Grand Haven station is located on the Grand River, within sight of Lake Michigan. The current facility was built in 1989.

Every year, Grand Haven hosts the Coast Guard festival, which began in the 1920s as a picnic for the men assigned to the station and grew into a full-fledged festival in the 1930s. Every year, thousands of people attend the event, including many of the senior admirals at the regional and national levels of the Coast Guard.

Though a cutter is no longer assigned to Grand Haven–the station operates several small boats–one of the most famed cutters in Coast Guard history, the Escanaba, once called Grand Haven home. The cutter was assigned to Grand Haven in the 1930s and was sent to the Atlantic Ocean during World War II. The cutter was sunk in 1943 by an enemy submarine while on convoy duty.

The Michigan state historical marker in Grand Haven tells the story of the station and the cutter:

Shipwrecks and the Coast Guard, Grand Haven

In Autumn 1929 raging storms sank four ships on Lake Michigan between Grand Haven and Milwaukee. Two went down with all hands - a total of seventy-seven men. The cargo ship Andaste departed Grand Haven for Chicago on September 9 and sank with her twenty-five man crew south of Holland. The car ferry Milwaukee sank en-route to Grand Haven on October 22 with a crew of fifty-two. Coast Guard personnel stationed in Grand Haven was hampered in search and rescue attempts by vessels unable to travel in heavy seas and the absence of ship-to-shore radios on the foundering ships. As a result, the U.S. Congress funded six additional Great Lakes Coast Guard cutters. Grand Haven became the home port of the Escanaba in December 1932.

The Escanaba, opposite side of above

On December 9, 1932, the 165-foot Coast Guard Cutter Escanaba arrived in Grand Haven, her home port until she was called to duty in World War II. On June 13, 1943, while escorting a convoy from Greenland to Newfoundland, the Escanaba was destroyed by an enemy submarine and sank in the North Atlantic. Only two crewmen survived. Grief-stricken, the citizens of Grand Haven organized a war bond campaign and raised over one million dollars in three months to pay for a "second Escanaba." Escanaba II was commissioned in 1946, but never visited Grand Haven. Escanaba III was commissioned in Grand Haven; she is now stationed in Boston. Each August, Grand Haven celebrates its relationship with the Coast Guard by hosting a festival that commemorates the founding of the United States Revenue Marine on August 4, 1790.

Chapter 59

The Coast Guard Cutter Buckthorn transits through the Soo Locks.
(U.S. Coast Guard)

Name: Sector Sault Ste. Marie
Location: Sault Ste. Marie
Established: 1916
Disposition: Still in operation
Owner: U.S.

Sector Sault Ste. Marie, located on the St. Mary's River near the famed Soo Locks, serves as both a station and as a sector office, the Coast Guard's next higher level of command. The station first opened in 1916 and Sault Ste. Marie has been a sector location since a 2005 Coast Guard reorganization.

Sault Ste. Marie is the homeport for two Coast Guard cutters, as well as several smaller boats. The cutters at Sault Ste. Marie are the 140-foot Katmai Bay and the 100-foot Buckthorn. The Katmai Bay, designated as an icebreaking tug, carries a crew of 17.

Commissioned in 1979, the Katmai Bay was the first of nine Bay-class cutters built for the Coast Guard. The Buckthorn is designated as an inland buoy tender, one of two 100-foot cutters and three 65-foot cutters so designated across the Coast Guard. The Buckthorn was commissioned in 1963 and carries a crew of 16.

Chapter 60

Selfridge Air National Guard Base, seen from the southwest in 2010.
(U.S. Air Force)

Thomas Selfridge, left, with Alexander Graham Bell. (U.S. Army)

Byron Q. Jones (U.S. Army)

Name: Selfridge Air National Guard Base, previously Selfridge Field, later, Selfridge Air Force Base
Location: Mount Clemens (Macomb County)
Established: 1917
Disposition: Still in use.
Owners: U.S.
Interesting fact: Known as "The Home of Generals."
Web site: www.127wg.ang.af.mil

One of the oldest continuously operating military air fields in the country–it depends somewhat on how you define the beginning of "operations," as well as the word "continuous" but Selfridge is easily among the 10 oldest no matter how one counts it and possibly even tops the list – the U.S. military took possession of Selfridge Field on July 1, 1917. On July 8, field commander Capt. Byron Q. Jones took the first flight and on July 16, pilot training at the base began. Selfridge Air National Guard Base is named for Lt. Thomas E. Selfridge. The early pilot is best known for being the first fatality of a airplane crash – it happened on Sept. 17, 1908, while on a flight with Orville Wright–but he was also the first U.S. military man to pilot an aircraft earlier that same year.

Flying at what is now Selfridge began around 1910 or so, when automobile magnate Henry B. Joy, president of the Packard Automobile Company, opened the private civilian Joy Aviation Field on the location. When the U.S. entered World War I, Joy convinced the Army to take his 300-acres-plus air field on a long-term lease. During World War I, more than 750 Army Air Service pilots and 1,000 aerial gunners received their initial training at the base. The pilots would then be shipped to France for final training and then combat assignments. After the war, the Army moved to close the base, prompting the first of a half dozen or so "save the base" campaigns over the ensuing century. Eventually the Army purchased the field and made a permanent base at the field. During World War II, the base's acreage was increased to its current size of 3,700-plus acres.

Following World War I, a number of world flight records were set at the base and Charles Lindbergh and Eddie Rickenbacker were among the aviators who trained at the base. It was also during the inter-war years that a number of young officers who later rose to key high command positions were assigned to the base, including Carl "Two-ey" Spaatz. Major Spaatz–who then spelled his name "Spatz" with one "a"–held his first command at Selfridge, as the commanding officer of the 1st Pursuit Group. In 1947, he would serve as the first chief of staff of the newly-created U.S. Air Force. Spaatz was one of three future USAF Chief of Staff to serve at Selfridge, helping to give the base the nickname "The Home of Generals."

Activity at the base greatly expanded during World War II as the nation again mobilized for war. During the war, an all-African American flying unit, the 332nd Fighter Group, began training at the base. Together with a number of units at other bases, the 332nd eventually became known as the Tuskegee Airmen. Despite bitter racial discrimination–including several high profile incidents at Selfridge–the Tuskegee Airmen helped lead the way to the desegregation of the U.S. military.

With the creation of the separate U.S. Air Force in 1947, Selfridge Field became Selfridge Air Force Base. The base continued as primarily a fighter aircraft base through 1971 when the active-duty Air Force left and turned the base over to the Michigan Air National Guard and the base took on the name Selfridge Air National Guard Base. Today, the base is home to units of the Air Force, Army, Navy, Marine Corps, Coast Guard, Border Patrol, Customs & Border Protection and other agencies. Aircraft assigned include A-10 Thunderbolt IIs (best known as the Warthog) and KC-135 Stratotankers, as well as several types of helicopters.

Contrary to some popular media accounts of the time, F-16 Fighting Falcon aircraft from the base were not dispatched to attempt to shoot down or otherwise intercept any high-jacked planes on Sept. 11, 2001. The base did have F-16s in the air that morning, but they were out of ammunition and low on fuel, returning from a training exercise at the air gunnery range in Grayling (see pages 16 and 34). The F-16s landed and re-armed, but were assigned to patrol the sky over Detroit, a mission that continued for several years.

An excellent air museum and vintage aircraft park exists at the base and is open to the public on weekends in April-October.

Here is the text of the state historical marker that exists at the Selfridge Military Air Museum:

Selfridge, Michigan's first real airport, began operations as a training base in July, 1917. It has progressed to a leading role in America's air arm. It is often called "The Home of the Generals" because Selfridge has been a springboard to success in the careers of 145 Air Force generals. It is named for Lt. Thomas E. Selfridge, the nation's first military pilot. In 1908 he was killed while flying with Orville Wright, becoming America's first military casualty of powered fight.

Chapter 61

Station Belle Isle (U.S. Coast Guard)

Name: Station Belle Isle
Location: Detroit (Wayne County)
Established: 1881.
Disposition: Still in operation
Owners: U.S.
Interesting fact: One of two Coast Guard locations in Detroit
Web site: http://www.uscg.mil/d9/sectdetroit/belleisle.asp

Detroit is one of the few communities in the nation with two Coast Guard locations inside the city limits, with operations on the mainland at Sector Detroit (see page 160), and on Belle Isle in the Detroit River. The property for Station Belle Isle was purchased by the federal government from the city of Detroit on April 6, 1881, for $1. The Belle Isle Light was built on the site and began operation on May 15, 1882.

In 1942, the small boast station was constructed on the island.

The excellent Dossin Great Lakes Museum, an arm of the Detroit Historical Society, is located nearby, also on Belle Isle.

Chapter 62

Station Charlevoix's 45-foot Response Boat-Medium is seen in summer 2013. (U.S. Coast Guard)

The U.S. Coast Guard Cutter Mesquite after running aground in 1989. (U.S. Coast Guard)

Name: Station Charlevoix
Location: Charlevoix (Charlevoix County)
Established: 1898.
Disposition: Still in operation
Owners: U.S.

One of several stations opened on the Great Lakes in 1898, Station Charlevoix was originally located on the Pine River Channel at Lake Michigan. In the early 1960s, it was moved to its current location at the channel's Lake Charlevoix end.

For about 50 years, Charlevoix was the homeport of a Coast Guard cutter. The 180-foot USCGC Sundew was assigned to the station from 1958 to 1977. In 1977, the Sundew was replaced in Charlevoix by the 180-foot USCGC Mesquite. The Mesquite remained in operation on the Upper Great Lakes until Dec. 4, 1989, when it was grounded on a reef off the Keweenaw Peninsula in Lake Superior. Efforts to free the ship failed and it was abandoned by her crew and later intentionally sunk and is now a part of the Keweenaw Underwater Preserve. Following the loss of the Mesquite, the 180-foot cutter Acacia was home-ported in Charlevoix. The Acacia was named for the original Acacia, which was the only vessel operated by the U.S. Lighthouse Service to be sunk in combat action during World War II. The USCGC Acacia was retired in 2006 after 62 years of service and since that time, no cutter has been permanently assigned to Charlevoix.

Chapter 63

Station Frankfort (U.S. Coast Guard)

Name: Station Frankfort
Location: Frankfort (Benzie County)
Established: 1887
Disposition: Still in operation
Owners: U.S.

The first lifesaving station in Frankfort opened in 1887. A Coast Guard presence (or a predecessor agency) has operated in the Frankfort area ever since. The current station, between Lake Michigan and Betsie Bay, was constructed in 2004.

Chapter 64

Station Harbor Beach (U.S. Coast Guard)

Name: Station Harbor Beach
Location: Harbor Beach (Huron County)
Established: 1881.
Disposition: Still in operation
Owners: U.S.
Web site: http://www.uscg.mil/d9/sectdetroit/harborbeach.asp

First opened in 1881 as "Sand Beach," the Harbor Beach station was moved to its current location in the small city of Harbor Beach in 1898. During World War II, the station was expanded to allow for the training of new Coast Guard recruits. The station was closed in 1973, but later was re-opened as a summer-only station. In 2004, the station was re-designated as a full-time, year-round station.

Chapter 65

Station Holland (U.S. Coast Guard)

Name: Station Holland
Location: Holland
Established: 1886
Disposition: Still in use
Owners: U.S.

Established in 1886, the station in Holland was originally located on the south side of Lake Macatawa. In 1996, a new station was built on the north side of the lake, near the Holland Sate Park.

Chapter 66

Station Ludington (U.S. Coast Guard)

Name: Station Ludington
Location: Ludington (Mason County)
Established: 1878
Disposition: Still in use
Owners: U.S.

The Ludington lifesaving station opened in 1878. The current 4,200-square foot facility was opened in 2004.

Chapter 67

Station Manistee (U.S. Coast Guard)

Name: Station Manistee
Location: Manistee (Manistee County)
Established: 1879
Disposition: Still in use
Owners: U.S.

Established in 1879, Station Manistee today operates two small boats. The station's current facility was opened in 2003.

Chapter 68

Name: Station Marquette
Location: Marquette (Marquette County)
Established: 1889
Disposition: Still in use
Owners: U.S.

Operating in the central portion of Lake Superior, Station Marquette has been in operation since 1889.

Chapter 69

Station Muskegon (U.S. Coast Guard)

Name: Station Muskegon / Air Facility Muskegon
Location: Muskegon (Muskegon County)
Established: late 1880s
Disposition: Still in use
Owners: U.S.
Interesting fact: Home to both a lifesaving station and an aids-to-navigation team.

In addition to serving as a small boat station, Muskegon, which opened for operations in the late 1880s, is also home to an Aids to Navigation–or ATON--team, tending buoys, lights and related markers along a roughly 200 mile stretch of Lake Michigan, from Indiana to Frankfort. The existing Muskegon station facility was built in 1927, with a major renovation in the late 1980s.

Air Facility Muskegon is separate from Station Muskegon. The air facility is a seasonal facility, staffed by personnel and a helicopter from Air Station Detroit during the recreational boating season, Memorial Day to Labor Day. The air facility is located at the Muskegon County Airport.

Chapter 70

Station Portage boat crews conduct training exercises aboard their 47-foot Motor Life Boat and 25-foot Response Boat-Small near Dollar Bay, Mich., in August 2012. (U.S. Coast Guard)

Name: Station Portage
Location: Dollar Bay (Houghton County)
Established: 1885
Disposition: Still in use
Owners: U.S.

Despite the building of a lighthouse in the Portage Canal near Houghton in 1874, a number of ships continued to wreck in the area, prompting the opening of a life saving station in 1885. The original station was built on the opposite side of the channel from the existing light in the canal. The current Station Portage opened in Dollar Bay in 1997.

In 1913, the lifesaving crews of the Portage station and the since-closed Eagle Harbor station, responded to the Nov. 8, shipwreck of the L.C. Waldo near Gull Rock Lighthouse, near the tip of the Keweenaw Peninsula. The crew of Waldo was rescued in a daring rescue during a brutal Lake Superior storm. Every member of both the Portage and Eagle Harbor stations were awarded the Gold Life-Saving Medal for Heroism as a result of the rescue–the only time in Coast Guard history the entire crew of a lifesaving station was so honored for a single event.

Chapter 71

The 225-foot Coast Guard Cutter Hollyhock has been assigned
to Station Port Huron since 2003. (U.S. Coast Guard)

The Coast Guard Cutter Bramble is seen shortly before
decommissioning in 2003. (U.S. Coast Guard)

Name: Station Port Huron
Location: Port Huron (St. Clair County)
Established: 1898.
Disposition: Still in operation
Owners: U.S.

The original lifeboat station in Port Huron was established in 1898. It was known as Station Lake View Beach and was located five miles north of the Fort Gratiot light. In 1931, three and a half acres of land surrounding Fort Gratiot Lighthouse was purchased by the government, and on April 13, 1932, Coast Guard Station Port Huron was officially opened. Station Lake View Beach was abandoned in 1946. In 2004, a new station facility was built and opened at Port Huron.

Since 2003, the 225-foot Juniper class cutter USCGC Hollyhock has been assigned to Port Huron. The Hollyhock is a multi-purpose vessel, which carries a crew of about 50. The Hollyhock is the second largest cutter assigned to Michigan, smaller only than the USCGC Mackinaw. It is one of two Juniper-class cutters assigned to the Great Lakes (the other being the USCGC Alder in Duluth, Minn.)

Port Huron was the home station to two notable ships now retired from service with the Coast Guard and one of its predecessor agencies, the U.S. Lighthouse Service: the Cutter Bramble and the Lightship Huron. The 180-foot Bramble was commissioned in 1944 and had a varied and storied career not only on the Great Lakes but also in the Caribbean and in the Pacific. In 1957, the Bramble was one of two Coast Guard cutters to make the Northwest Passage, traveling along the frigid northern shore of Canada from the Pacific to the Atlantic. After that mission, the ship was assigned to Detroit in 1962 and then to Port Huron in 1975. Through the late 1980s and most of the 1990s, the ship would spend the winter months on various assignments in the Caribbean and then return to Port Huron in the summers. The ship was decommissioned in 2003 and was used for a time as a museum ship as part of the Port Huron Museum. The museum sold the ship to a private party in 2013, though it remains in Port Huron. The Lightship Huron was essentially a floating, portable light house. The 97-foot vessel was launched in 1920 and remained in service through Aug. 25, 1970, with a home port in Port Huron during all of that time. After the ship was decommissioned, the ownership of it was transferred to the city of Port Huron. Today, it is operated as part of the Port Huron Museum system and is open for tours.

Here is the text of a Michigan state historical marker in Port Huron:

Huron Lightship

Commissioned in 1921, the Huron began service as a relief vessel for other Great Lakes lightships. She is ninety-seven feet long, twenty-four feet in beam, and carried a crew of eleven. On clear nights her beacon could be seen for fourteen miles. After serving in northern Lake Michigan, the Huron was assigned to the Corsica Shoals in 1935. These shallow waters, six miles north of Port Huron, were the scene of frequent groundings by lake freighters in the late nineteenth century. A lightship station had been established there in 1893, since the manned ships were more reliable than lighted buoys. After 1940 the Huron was the only lightship on the Great Lakes. Retired from Coast Guard Service in 1970, she was presented to the City of Port Huron in 1971.

Chapter 72

Station Saginaw River (U.S. Coast Guard)

Name: Station Saginaw River
Location: Essexville (Bay County)
Established: 1847 / late 1880s
Disposition: Still in operation
Owners: U.S.

The federal government established a lighthouse at the Saginaw River in 1842 on land ceded to the U.S. by the Chippewa Native American tribe. In the late 1880s, a life saving station was also established nearby. In 1980, the Coast Guard station moved to its present location in Essexville. Today, as a small boat station, it is home to about 20 Coast Guard personnel.

Chapter 73

Station St. Clair Shores (U.S. Coast Guard)

Name: Station St. Clair Shores
Location: St. Clair Shores (Macomb County)
Established: 1954
Disposition: Still in operation
Owners: U.S.

Though it has one of the smallest areas of responsibility in the U.S. Coast Guard, Station St. Clair Shores generally ranks in the top 5 stations in the nations in a number of statistics, including search and rescue operations and law enforcement-related operations.

The station is located near the Blossom Heath community center along the "Nautical Mile" in St. Clair Shores. Blossom Heath was a notorious speak-easy and transportation hub for international booze runners during the U.S. prohibition period of the 1920s.

Station St. Clair Shores was established in 1954. The station's current building was constructed in 1990. In addition the approximately two dozen assigned active duty Coast Guard personnel, the station is supported by about two dozen members of the Coast Guard Reserve and a couple hundred members of the volunteer Coast Guard Auxiliary and a contingent of the volunteer U.S. Power Squadron, a boater safety organization. Station St. Clair Shores is the base of operations for the marine unit of the Macomb County Sheriff's Department, which operates during the summer boating season.

Chapter 74

Station St. Ignace (U.S. Coast Guard)

Name: Station St. Ignace
Location: St. Ignace (Mackinac County)
Established: late 1880s
Disposition: Still in use
Owners: U.S.
Interesting fact: Small boat station and aids to navigation team

Station St. Ignace conducts a variety of missions in and around the Straits of Mackinac. It is also the home to a navigation team.

Chapter 75

A life saving crew is seen during a training exercise in this photo,
likely from the 1920s, taken at Station St. Joseph. (U.S. Coast Guard)

Name: Station St. Joseph
Location: St. Joseph (St. Joseph County)
Established: 1874
Disposition: Still in use
Owners: U.S.

Station St. Joseph was one of the earliest stations on the Great
Lakes, established in 1874. The current facility underwent a major
renovation in 1997.

Chapter 76

Station Tawas (U.S. Coast Guard)

Name: Station Tawas
Location: East Tawas (Iosco County)
Established: 1876
Disposition: Still in use
Owners: U.S.
Interesting fact: Was originally known as Ottawa Point station.

First opened in 1876 as the Ottawa Point station, the current building at the station dates from 1919. The station has also been informally known as the Near Light Lake Huron.

Chapter 77

Name: Tri-City Army Air Field
Location: Freeland (Saginaw County)
Year Built: 1941
Disposition: In operation at MBS International Airport
Owner: U.S.
Interesting fact: Never put into active service as a military air field, but was housed to house German Prisoners of War.

Local governmental leaders began planning for a civilian airport in the Saginaw / Bay City / Midland region in the 1930s. By the time the first property was purchased for the airport, in 1941, the U.S. was on the brink of war and the airport was taken over by the War Department for use. Despite this, Tri-City Army Air Field was never put into regular use as a military air field. It did serve another purpose, however: it was one of several locations around the state to be used to house Prisoners of War. Thousands of German POWs spent some part of the war at Tr-City.

After the war, the airport was turned back over to local governmental control and operated as Tri-City Airport for many years. In the 1990s, the name of the airport was changed to MBS International to avoid name confusion with other "tri-city" regions in the U.S.

Chapter 78

The U.S.S. Silversides is seen dockside with all
her flags flying in Muskegon. (U.S. Navy)

Name: U.S.S. Silversides
Location: Muskegon (Muskegon County)
Established: Commissioned 1942.
Disposition: Decommissioned 1969. Now used as a museum ship.
Owners: U.S.
Interesting fact: Third most successful U.S. submarine in World War II in terms of enemy ships sunk.

While certainly not a fort or other military installation, the USS Silversides deserves inclusion in this list for its notable war record and its decades-long residency tied up alongside the Great Lakes Naval Memorial & Museum in Muskegon.

The Silversides is a World War II Gato-class submarine that served on 14 patrols during that war and sunk 23 enemy ships. The

Silversides ranked third among American submarines in World War II in terms of ships sunk and second in terms of total tonnage of enemy shipping sunk. The Silversides won 12 battle stars for World War II service and was awarded the Presidential Unit Citation. The Silverside was on active duty service from 1942 to 1969.

After spending about 20 years as a museum ship operated by several different organizations in Chicago, Silversides was moved to Muskegon in 1987 as the centerpiece of the museum in Muskegon. The ship is open for tours and can accommodate Scouts and similar groups for overnight stays. The Silversides is joined at the Muskegon museum by the 125-foot Coast Guard cutter McLane, which was launched in 1925 and decommissioned in 1969. The McLane is also open for tours.

While neither the Silversides nor the McLane have a direct Michigan tie, they are a must-see attraction for those interested in military history.

Chapter 79

Name: Wayne Stockade
Location: Monroe (Monroe County)
Established: 1796
Disposition: Burned by the British, 1812.
Owners: U.S.
Interesting fact: May have been the site of the first official U.S. flag to be flown over modern-day Michigan, in 1796.

The Wayne Stockade, located in modern-day downtown Monroe, was established in 1806, when a blockhouse, surrounded by a wooden palisades, was built. A blockhouse was originally established on the location in 1796 by local settlers. According to Monroe sources, the first U.S. flag to fly over what is today the state of Michigan flew over that stockade in 1796. The facility was located near the modern intersection of Elm Street and Monroe Avenue.

In 1806, Congress ordered the stockade to be built in Monroe, along with some other locations, as a "defense against Indians."

In 1812, when the U.S. declared war against the British in the War of 1812, part of General William Hull's Army of the Northwest was garrisoned at the stockade. Hull, who was concurrently serving as Michigan's territorial governor, gathered his forces with a plan to attack the British in Ontario, across the Detroit River from Detroit. Instead, facing British artillery and other forces, Hull surrendered Detroit–and by extension the rest of Michigan–to the British. Back in Monroe, at the Wayne Stockade, Capt. Henry Brush, who was in command of the remaining garrison, refused to surrender the facility to the British. An overwhelming British force took possession of the Stockade and, on Sept. 2, 1812, burned it to the ground.

Today, a statue of one of Monroe's most famed former residents, Gen. George Armstrong Custer, stands on the grounds near the former site of the Wayne Stockade.

Chapter 80

B-24 Liberators are seen on the production line in this 1944 photo
At the Willow Run plant. (U.S. Army)

Name: Willow Run Air Force Station / Willow Run Plant
Location: Ypsilanti (Washtenaw County)
Established: (As Air Force Station) 1951
Disposition: Closed 1959. Sold to University of Michigan, later sold to Wayne County Airport Authority. Many buildings still exist
Owners: U.S.
Interesting fact: One of several radar facilities across the state during the Cold War era.
Web site: www.yankeeairmuseum.org

While it would later serve as a formal Air Force Station, the Willow Run name will likely be forever most associated with the awesome display of industrial power exhibited there during World War II. The manufacturing plant at the site was a key aircraft production hub during the war. At the peak of operations, workers at the plant–many of them women who later became collectively known as Rosie the Riveter–produced one B-24 Liberator aircraft every 63 minutes, with operations continuing 24 hours per day, seven days per week. During the war, 6,972 B-24 were built at the plant and 1,893 parts kits were built for final assembly elsewhere, for total production of 8,685 aircraft from September 1942 to April 1945.

Though controlled by the Ford Motor Company, during the war the plant was owned by the federal Defense Plant Corp. The 484th Base Headquarters and Base Squadron and various other Army Air Forces units had a presence at the plant during World War II. With the conclusion of the war in 1945, the plant was returned to Ford ownership.

In 1951, the Air Force returned to the Willow Run Airport and established Willow Run Air Force Station, making it the headquarters of the 30th Air Division. The Air Force Station was one of about a half dozen that operated in the state during the Cold War era. In April 1959, the 30th AD was reassigned to Wisconsin and the Air Force closed its Willow Run operations, selling its buildings there to the University of Michigan. The university later sold its holdings there to the Wayne County Airport Authority. Many of the original Air Force Station buildings still exist.

The Willow Run Airport is the site of the Yankee Air Museum, which operates an impressive collection of historic aircraft and other artifacts. Among the highlights of the museum's operation are several World War II-era bomber aircraft which remain flightworthy. Museum visitors can arrange to take flights aboard several of the vintage World War II-era aircraft operated at the museum, with advance registration.

Here is the text of the Michigan State Historical Marker at the Willow Run Airport (a separate marker highlights the Willow Run plant's history as an auto plant):

After entering World War II in 1941, America desperately needed military equipment and supplies. The Ford Motor Company had begun building this factory in April 1941. Outstanding industrial architect Albert Kahn designed Willow Run, one of the largest manufacturing plants under one roof in the world. Completed in early 1942, this bulwark of the "Arsenal of Democracy" produced 8685 B-24 Liberator Bombers and had a peak employment of 42,000 men and women. After the war, the newly formed Kaiser-Frazer Corporation--in an unsuccessful effort to create a large scale automotive empire--occupied this plant. Here the company manufactured the first of 739,039 passenger cars, as well as military aircraft. In 1953 Kaiser-Frazer transferred its diminishing operations from Willow Run to Toledo, Ohio, and Argentina.

Chapter 81

A B-52 Stratofortress is seen at Wurtsmith Air Force Base
in this 1960s-era photo. (U.S. Air Force)

Paul B. Wurtsmith (U.S. Air Force)

Name: Wurtsmith Air Force Base / Camp Skeel / Oscoda
Army Air Field

Location: Oscoda (Oscoda County)
Established: 1923
Disposition: Closed 1993. Now used for a variety of commercial uses and as an airport.
Owners: U.S.

The base that eventually came to be known as Wurtsmith Air Force Base is located on the shores of Lake Van Ettan near Oscoda in Iosco County in northeast Michigan. The base was first utilized in the early winter months of 1923 when pilots and Airmen from the 1st Pursuit Group at Selfridge Field utilized the frozen lake as a landing field for temporary winter maneuvers. The 1923 maneuvers were among the most extensive air war games held in the early years of the U.S. Army's Air Corps. Despite the cold winds and harsh weather conditions, the pilots reported a warm welcome from the people of Oscoda and began returning to the field for winter maneuvers on a mostly annual basis until World War II. In 1924, the field was named Camp Skeel in honor of Capt. Burt Skeel, a deceased former pilot of the First Pursuit Group.

With the outbreak of World War II, three concrete runways were installed at the field and it was renamed Oscoda Army Air Field. During the war, the 100th Base HQ and Air Base Squadron was activated as the host unit. The field had various uses during the war. Initially it was tasked with providing air defense to the shipping channels at Sault Ste. Marie and St. Ignace. When that assignment was given to air units stationed at Alpena and other points north, Oscoda later became the home of the 332nd Fighter Group. The 332nd was one of the units that later collectively came to be known as the Tuskegee Airmen, the all-Black unit of pilots and mechanics. The unit had been based at Selfridge, but was reassigned to Oscoda due to escalating racial tensions at Selfridge. The Group later deployed to great success in the European Command during the war. Later still, the base was used as a training center for the Free French Air Force, a group of French personnel who escaped from Nazi-controlled France and later returned to fight for the liberation of their home country.

After World War II, the base was mostly vacated for the last half of the 1940s, though it did host an Air Force radar station for a brief period.

In 1951, the base was re-activated. New, larger runways were installed, and the 63rd Fighter Interceptor Group, flying the F-86 Sabre, was assigned to the base. Later upgrades included the use of the F-89 Scorpion, the F-102 Delta Dagger and the F-106 Delta Dart.

In 1960, the base was transferred from the Air Defense Command to the Strategic Air Command. The 40th Air Division was transferred to the base and the 379th Bombardment Wing was the host unit at the base, supported by the 920th Air Refueling Group. The 379th and 920th flew the B-52 Stratofortress and the KC-135 Stratotanker, a bomber and aerial refueler, respectively. In the early 1980s, the base was also selected to serve as the home base of a railroad-based Intercontinental Ballistic Missile System, but that system was never fielded due to political and budgetary concerns.

With the collapse of the Soviet Union in the late 1980s and a related reduction in nuclear arms–the B-52 was a nuclear capable bomber, though under Air Force policy the presence of nuclear weapons at Wurtsmith, or any other base, has never been officially confirmed nor denied–Wurtsmith was declared surplus in a round of base closings. The base was closed in 1993. The runways at the base are now used as a local regional airport. A variety of residential, governmental and commercial uses now take place on the former base, though the level of activity at the base is nowhere near its high point during the air base years. At its height, the base included more than 4,600 acres and had several thousand Airmen assigned. A small museum exists on the grounds of the former base.

Burt Skeel briefly held command of the 27th Pursuit Squadron, part of the First Pursuit Group, at Selfridge Field in the early 1920s. In 1923, he won the Mitchell Trophy Race in St. Louis, Mo., flying a MB-3A at a top speed of 161 miles per hour. The following year, just days before he was to enter the Pulitzer Trophy

Race that fall at Wilbur Wright Field in Dayton, Ohio, Skeel was speed testing a Curtiss aircraft when it broke up in flight on Oct. 4, 1924. Skeel, flying without a parachute as was the norm at the time, died in the resulting crash

Wurtsmith, a native of Detroit, enlisted with the famed 94th Pursuit Squadron–known as the "Hat in the Ring" squadron – at Selfridge Field (see page 168) in 1928. During World War II, he was in command of V Fighter Command, the fighter aircraft arm in Fifth Air Force, involved extensively with the defense of Australia. In the closing days of the war, Wurtsmith commanded 13th Air Force in the Pacific theater. After the war, in September 1946, he assumed command of 8th Air Force, as part of Strategic Air Command. Just days later, on Sept. 13, 1946, Wurtsmith was killed when the B-25 Mitchell he was flying from Selfridge Field to MacDill AFB in Florida crashed into a mountain in North Carolina. The base in Oscoda was renamed in Wurtsmith's honor shortly thereafter.

Chapter 82

Name: Ypsilanti Barracks
Location: Ypsilanti (Washtenaw County)
Established: 1861
Disposition: Only used for military purposes in 1861
Owners: U.S.
Interesting fact: Civil War mustering site

One of numerous Civil War mustering locations across the state, the Ypsilanti Barracks, otherwise known as the Thompson Block, was a single commercial building in downtown Ypsilanti. It was only used for military purposes for a few months in 1861.

There is a Michigan state historical marker on the site today.

Ypsilanti Barracks

When the Civil War began in 1861, this corner site housed a commercial building called the Norris Block. Its location across the street from the railroad station made it an ideal place for short-term lodging for enlistees waiting to be sent off to battle, and locals soon dubbed it The Barracks. The Ypsilanti Light Guard, a local militia company that became Company H, First Michigan Infantry, stayed here in the spring of 1861. They mustered in Detroit on May 1 and arrived in Washington, D.C., on May 16. Recruits for the Fourteenth Michigan Infantry, including 129 men from Washtenaw County, spent six months here from September 1861 to February 1862 while the regiments ranks were filled. The Fourteenth first saw action as part of the siege of Corinth, Mississippi.

Ypsilanti in the Civil War (opposite side of above)

More than 4,000 soldiers from Washtenaw County served during the Civil War. Hundreds bivouacked here, in the Nor-

ris Block, before mustering into service. More than thirty men who were students or graduates of the Michigan State Normal School (now Eastern Michigan University) joined Company E of the Seventeenth Michigan Infantry in 1862. Their first action was at South Mountain in Maryland. In December 1863, the First Michigan Colored Infantry stopped here as part of its state-wide recruiting drive. In 1902 veterans of the Twenty-Seventh Michigan Infantry held their reunion here. Since the 1880s this site has been known as the Thompson Block and has had a variety of commercial uses.

Appendix A:
What is a (an)…?

A few words about some of the terms used for the various military installations that have existed in Michigan might be helpful.

The most common terms used to describe Michigan's military locations are fort, camp, base, station, field, armory and arsenal. Some of the terms are almost interchangeable; some vary by era and/or by the policy of the nation that first operated the location in question; and periodically the naming conventions do not follow the general guidelines of the time of when the name was first applied. Still, there are some rough definitions that can be applied to those terms.

Armory: *The modern usage of this term is as a training and gathering center for National Guard and/or military reserve personnel. Perhaps the best known armories in Michigan are the Detroit Light Guard Armory and the relatively recently closed Brodhead Naval Armory in Detroit. In other contexts, the word Armory relates to a facility where weapons are made or stored, such as the original Detroit Arsenal in Dearborn.*

Arsenal: *A location where weapons and ammunition are stored and/or manufactured. Though large stores of weapons are neither kept nor manufactured there, the modern-day Detroit Arsenal is a headquarters center for the management of many U.S. Army weapons systems.*

Base: *This is kind of a catch-all phrase, though it is now used specifically to designate a major Air Force facility. Gen-*

erally speaking, most Air Fields became Air Force Bases after World War II. Some fields were named Army Air Forces Base in the early days of World War II. Selfridge Field did not become Selfridge Air Force Base until 1947, when the Air Force became a separate service.

*   **Camp:** *Primarily developed as temporary war-time facilities, a number of Michigan camps were created as part of the build-up for the Civil War and World War I, such as Camp Butler. The word "camp" has been used to identify the location of military forces at least since the 1520s in France. Today, the most notable camp in Michigan is the National Guard training center at Camp Grayling.*

*   **Field:** *All Army air fields were referred to as Fields until World War II, when the word Base began to replace it. In 1947, when the Air Force became a separate service, all remaining fields were re-designated as bases. The Army continues to call its air operations centers "Fields," such as the Grayling Army Air Field, which is a part of Camp Grayling.*

*   **Fort:** *In regard to U.S.-created facilities, the War Department issued the following directive on Feb. 8, 1832: "All new posts which may be hereafter established, will receive their names from the War Department, and be announced in General Orders from the Headquarters of the Army." Army leadership also stated at the time that a camp was to be considered a temporary location and a fort was a permanent installation. Obviously this guideline does not always apply, as Michigan's Camp Grayling is now more than 100 years old. The word fort, or fortification, comes from the Latin word*

"fortis" which means "strong." Most forts have (or had) a structure that was used as part of the defense of the location, such as the wooden stockade around Fort Michilimackinac.

__Station:__ This word means different things in different military contexts. For the U.S. Coast Guard, virtually every facility, other than stand-alone lighthouses, are referred to as stations, be they locations where cutters and other boats are located or the air stations in Detroit (Selfridge ANGB) or Traverse City. The Navy took a similar approach and called its only permanent major facility in Michigan the Grosse Ile Naval Air Station. For the Air Force, installations known as Air Force Stations were locations where the primary mission was not flying and, in fact, a runway may not even have been a part of the infrastructure. Rather, Air Force Stations were primarily radar locations during the early part of the Cold War era.

Other terms used in this book:

__Blockhouse:__ A small, often two-story structure, generally made of heavy wood or logs, that serves as the defensive strong point. The building is generally square and often features a second story that is slightly larger than the main floor. Generally the blockhouse contains no offices or other interior features, but was to be used strictly as a defensive location for soldiers, with small windows or slits, through which weapons could be fired.

__Earthworks:__ An embankment made of earth, sometimes reinforced with wood or rocks, used as a fortification.

Palisade: *A fence or wall made from wooden stakes or logs. Used interchangeably with Stockade.*

Stockade: *Any permanent fence, wall or similar barricade made of logs or wooden posts driven into the ground. Used interchangeably with Stockade.*

Appendix B:

Coast Guard Operations in Michigan

Likely the best known ship of the modern-era on the Great Lakes was the original icebreaker Mackinaw. This ship was decommissioned in 2006 after 62 years of operation on the Great Lakes. It was replaced by a smaller, more efficient icebreaker, also named Mackinaw. (U.S. Coast Guard)

Coast Guard Cutters

Six U.S. Coast Guard cutters are stationed in Michigan. All of the Coast Guard stations in Michigan are assigned a variety of "small boats" to perform their various search and rescue, law enforcement and other tasks. A cutter is defined as having a length of 65 feet or greater and living accommodations onboard for the crew.

Of the following cutters assigned to Michigan, the Bay class cutters are 140 feet long with a crew of 17. The Buckthorn is 100 feet long and has a crew of 16. The Mackinaw carries a crew of 55 and is 240 feet long. The existing cutter Mackinaw is the second ship of that name to serve the Great Lakes. The first Mackinaw was launched in 1944 in response to the need to keep Great Lakes shipping operating year-round during World War II. The 290-foot Mackinaw (WAGB-83) served for more than 60 years and was decommissioned in 2006 and replaced by the newer, smaller, more efficient ship. The original Mackinaw is now a museum ship in Mackinaw City.

Michigan homeports of Coast Guard cutters
Cheboygan: USCGC Mackinaw
Detroit: USCGC Bristol Bay
Port Huron: USCGC Hollyhock
St. Ignace: USCGC Biscayne Bay
Sault Ste. Marie: USCGC Buckthorn
Sault Ste. Marie: USCGC Katmai Bay

Here is the text of the Michigan state historical marker that honors the Mackinaw:

Cutter Mackinaw, Mackinaw City

Built in 1944 at a cost of $10 million, U.S. Coast Guard cutter MACKINAW had six ten-cylinder engines that enabled it to cut through several feet of lake ice. The powerful steel ice-breaker was commissioned during World War II to aid year-round navigation so freighters could carry raw materials for war production. For sixty-two years MACKINAW left its home port of Cheboygan to open or extend the navigation season, clear the shipping lanes, or free vessels that were stuck in the ice. MACKINAW was unsurpassed in size and capability among icebreakers. When the coast guard decommissioned the vessel in 2006, it was given to the Icebreaker Mackinaw Maritime Museum.

Coast Guard Stations

The U.S. Coast Guard has a long and diverse history of service on the Great Lakes. Nationally, the Coast Guard traces its history to the commissioning of several "revenue cutters" by President George Washington in 1790. The action led to the creation of the U.S. Revenue Cutter Service. In 1915, Congress merged the Revenue Cutter Service with the U.S. Life-Saving Service and dubbed the new agency the U.S. Coast Guard. In 1936, the Lighthouse Service was folded into the Coast Guard and in 1946 the Bureau of Marine Inspection & Navigation was also added. In 2003, the Coast Guard became an agency of the new Dept. of Homeland Security.

The following is a list of former Coast Guard Stations, operated by the Coast Guard or its predecessor organizations, which existed in Michigan with their opening and closing dates. In many cases, while the "station" was closed, an active Coast Guard-operated light or light house continued in operation for many years after the closing of the station, many to the present day.

Station	Opened	Closed
Beaver Island	1875	1922
Bois Blanc Island	1890	1956
Charleviox	1899	circa 1960s
Crisp Point (Munising)	1876	1950s
Deer Park	1876	1955
Eagle Harbor	1905	1940s?
Grand Point AuSable	1876	1954
Grindstone City	1878	1939
Hammond Bay (Rogers City)	1876	1968
Lakeview Beach (Lakeport)	1898	1946
Middle Island (Marquette)	circa 1879	1950s
North Manitou Island	1876	1939
Pentwater	1886	early 1960s
Point Betsie (Frankfort)	1875	1946

Here is the text of a Michigan state historical marker that honors the former Two-Hearted River station:

Life Saving Station, Luce County

Here stood the Two-Hearted River Life Saving Station, built in 1876. This station, like many others on the Great Lakes, was of the second class--erected at a cost of $4,790 and manned by volunteer crews. The facility, a simple two-story building with a small lookout tower, housed a lifeboat and other necessary equipment for recovering endangered sailors. An average crew consisted of six to eight experienced surfmen. In 1915 the Life Saving Service was integrated into the U.S. Coast Guard.

Several shipwrecks occurred near the mouth of the Two-Hearted River, also referred to as the Twin River and the Big Two Hearted River. Among these were the Cleveland (1864), the W. W. Arnold (1869), and the Sumatra (1875). After construction of the life saving station here in 1876, the lifesavers were responsible for brave rescues in the Satellite (1879) and the Phineas S. Marsh (1896) disasters. The station was decommissioned in the 1930s and the structure was razed in 1944.

Nike missiles on launchers at Selfridge Air Force Base in the middle 950s. An inert Nike missile is on display at the Selfridge Military Air Museum at Selfridge Air National Guard Base. (U.S. Air Force)

Appendix C:

Michigan's Cold War Missile Sites[1]

For more than a quarter century, through the coldest years of the Cold War, the people of the Detroit region--and the all-important industrial might of the Motor City--were protected by their local,

---

[1] This appendix has been modified and updated from an article originally written by the author in 2008 and published in a newsletter of the Michigan Air National Guard. The original article exists in the public domain.

neighborhood missile system.

Already, the Army's Nike and Ajax missiles have been gone longer than they were here. Since the missiles were decommissioned, the nation has long since moved beyond the Cold War, passed through a period dubbed the "Peace Dividend" by the first President Bush and, since the terror attacks of Sept. 11, 2001, has been spent a decade or so engaged in the Global War on Terror and has now moving on to the post-Iraq/Afghanistan era. But for 26 years, from 1948 to 1974, the Army and its collection of anti-aircraft guns and surface-to-air missiles kept the Detroit area and other U.S. cities safe from the threat of Soviet bombers. The A-A guns were in several locations around the Detroit region, roughly from 1952 to 1957, when they were replaced by the missiles.

"[The missiles were] the last line of defense against attacking enemy aircraft," U.S. Army Col. Stephen P. Moeller wrote in "Vigilant and Invincible," a history of the Army's Air Defense Command, or ARADCOM, which appeared in the May/June 1995 issue of ADA (Air Defense Artillery) Magazine. "When deterrence became a part of the United States' national strategy, ARADCOM was key and essential to that effort. Was it successful? Measured by the number of attacks on the United States by the Soviets in the 24 years of ARADCOM's existence, it was 100 percent so."

Recognizing the importance of the industrial muscle of Detroit, NORAD protected the region using the Army's ARADCOM and fighter jets on 24-hour alert at Selfridge Air National Guard Base (then called Selfridge Air Force Base) in Macomb County and at other bases in northern Michigan.

An article in the Mount Clemens (Mich.) Monitor Leader, a predecessor of today's Macomb Daily newspaper, marked the 12th anniversary of the 516th Anti-Aircraft Missile Battalion at Selfridge AFB on Sept. 20, 1955, and explained how the missiles operated:

"When the battalion was formed in 1948, anti-aircraft defense was about as complicated as a pheasant hunt," reporter Simon O'Shea wrote in the article. With the Nike system (in place in 1955), "Radio signals will relentlessly direct the guided missiles to a deadly rendezvous with the enemy."

According to the plan at the time, fighters from Selfridge and other bases around the country would first be dispatched to intercept any possible attack. Any bombers that slipped through and got to within 150 miles of the city were to be knocked out by the 34-foot long, one-ton missile. A direct hit was not considered necessary - a near miss was expected to be enough to knock the enemy out of the sky. Clearly, during the 1955 anniversary celebration, the Army and the Air Force made a believer out of O'Shea, the reporter.

"The deadly accuracy and explosive power of the fantastic missiles guided to their targets by radar could prove a vital force in defending the whole metropolitan area and the mighty air force base," he wrote at the time.

Today, the Military Air Museum at Selfridge has two old and deactivated ("but lovingly restored and cared for") missiles on display at the museum's air park, a SAM-A-7 Nike Ajax and a SAM-N-25 Nike Hercules.

For the most part, there is little evidence of the old missile system at any of the Detroit area locations where they once were located. One site is now a parking lot at Oakland University's Auburn Hills campus; at another, the Detroit Police Department now operates a training center. One site was located at Detroit Metro Airport, another was on Belle Isle and a total of three were located at Selfridge.

All of the sites in the Detroit region were initially operated by units of the regular U.S. Army and equipped with Nike Ajax missiles. By around 1963, units of the Michigan Army National Guard had replaced most of the active-duty soldiers at the sites and the upgraded Nike Hercules missile had been installed at the sites.

NORAD and the military eventually determined that the Air Force fighter jets on alert at various bases, coupled with improving early warning radar systems, were adequate to defend the nation's largest cities, according to Moeller's article. The missile system was cut back in 1971, and then in 1974 the Army de-activated all the missile sites in the Detroit region and across the nation, save for a few that operated in southern Florida for another half-dozen years.

The sites listed below with "A-A guns" each had a battery of four 90mm guns. Some locations also had barracks and other support buildings.

Site locations (all in southeastern Michigan):

D-06: Utica. Now part of Riverbends Park, this site contained 20 Ajax missiles, later replaced by 12 Hercules Missiles. Active 1955-April 1974

D-14: Selfridge Air Force Base. Active 1955-63. 20 Ajax missiles.

D-15DC: Selfridge Air Force Base. Operated by the regular Army for its entire operation, this site was the first missile site to be activated and second from last to be decommissioned in the Detroit area. It was in operation from 1954-June 1974. The "missile master" building was demolished in 2005, but several Nike-related buildings remain at Selfridge and are used as the Selfridge Military Air Museum. Number of missiles unknown.

D-16: Selfridge Air Force Base. September 1958-June 1971. 20 Ajax/12 Hercules missiles

D-17: Rural St. Clair County, east of Marine City on Short Cut Road. A-A guns, 1952-57.Replaced by 30 Ajax missiles, June 1957-February 1963.

D-23: Detroit, Ford Brush Park. Had elements at City Airport and on Belle Isle. April 1955-December 1960.20 Ajax missiles.

D-26: Detroit, Maheras-Gentry Park. Had elements on Belle Isle. April 1955-November 1968.20 Ajax/Hercules.

D-50: Detroit. 6301 West Jefferson.1953-55. A-A guns.

D-51: Grosse Ile. Location at the Grosse Ile Airport and near Groh and East River roads. A-A Guns: 1952. Ajax missiles: January 1955 February 1963.

D-54-55. A double-sized site, with two nearby locations in **Riverview.** The launcher area is now a city park used as soccer fields. January 1955 February 1963.60 Ajax missiles. One small former building from the control site is used as a community center.

D-57: Newport. Built on what had been Newport Naval Air Station during World War II, this Monroe County location is perhaps the most complete remaining Nike site in the state. Most of the buildings that were used at the launch control site remain intact, include some radar towers. Part of the area continues to be owned by the Michigan Army National Guard. January 1955-February 1963.30 Ajax missiles.

D-58: Newport. Co-located by D-57. It also has several buildings remaining. June 1959-April 1974.30 Ajax/18 Hercules missiles. Briefly the site of A-A guns, 1955.

D-61: Detroit Metro Airport, Romulus. The location of the site is now a taxiway at the airport. June 1957-June 1971.30 Ajax/18 Hercules missiles.

D-62: Dearborn. At the intersection of Greenfield Road and Dearborn Street. No weapons, but a headquarters building was located here. 1953-55.

D-69: Detroit, what is now River Rouge Park. January 1955-February 1963.20 Ajax missiles.

D-72: Detroit. At corner of Mark Twain and Belton streets.1952-55. A-A guns.

D-86: Bingham Farms. Some of the former buildings were later used now as an Army Reserve site. June 1957-February 1963.30 Ajax missiles.

D-87: Commerce Township. Many of the buildings at this site remain intact and have since been refurbished for use as a recreation site operated by the Michigan Dept. of Natural Resources. It was the last Detroit area site to be decommissioned. January 1955-November 1974.30 Ajax/18 Hercules missiles.

D-90: Ferndale. In what is now Harding Park.1954-56. A-A guns.

D-91: Hazel Park, near Ryan and 10 Mile roads.1952-56. A-A guns.

D-97: Auburn Hills. Now the site of Oakland Community College's Auburn Hills campus. 1955-February 1963.30 Ajax missiles.

The site numbers are unclear for the following locations.

Fort Wayne, Detroit. A-A guns. Also had an administrative support operation. 1955

Detroit, corner of Crusade and Novara streets, now the Heilmann Recreation Center. 1952-57

Dearborn, at Southfield and Ford Roads. 1955

The following locations had A-A guns in 1955, but the dates the guns were placed or removed, as well as the location numbers, are unknown:

Warren: at Hoover Road and Hupp.

Grosse Pointe Farms: at present-day Brownell Middle School.

Grosse Pointe Park: at end of Three Mile Drive.

Detroit: at Van Antwerp Park, at Wyoming Ave. and St. Martins.

Ecorse: at West Jefferson Ave. and Westfield Road.

Here is the test for a Michigan state historical marker that recognizes the site of the D-06 missile site:

Utica Nike Base, Shelby Township

During the 1950s the U.S. Army developed its Nike anti-aircraft program. The conventional Nike Ajax guided missile and its nuclear-capable successor, Hercules, provided America's cities with a "last line of defense" against attack by Soviet long-range bombers carrying atomic warheads. The Detroit region's Nike perimeter included fifteen missile bases. The Utica site comprised a launch facility (located one-half mile west of here) and an Integrated Fire Control center/administrative area (located one-third mile south). Army and Michigan National Guard units manned the site from 1955 until 1974, when it closed. The enemy bombers had been replaced by intercontinental ballistic missiles, a new threat against which the Nike system would be useless.

Appendix D:
Armories & Reserve Centers

Michigan National Guard Armories are generally relatively small, single building complexes, were local companies of the National Guard gather for monthly meetings. Large-scale training often takes place at Camp Grayling or other major facilities.

National Guard armories:
Albion
Alma
Alpena Combat Readiness Training Center
Baraga
Bay City
Big Rapids
Cadillac
Calumet
Camp Grayling
Charlotte
Cheboygan
Corunna
Detroit / Light Guard Armory
Detroit / Olympia Armory
Flint
Fort Custer
Gladstone
Grand Ledge
Grand Rapids
Greenville
Howell
Iron River
Ironwood
Ishpeming
Jackson

Kalamazoo
Kingsford
Lansing (Joint Forces Headquarters)
Lapeer
Manistee
Marquette
Midland
Montague
Pontiac
Port Huron
Saginaw
Sault Ste. Marie
Selfridge ANGB
Sturgis
Taylor
Wyoming
Ypsilanti

Here is the text for the Michigan state historical marker at the armory in Wyoming, Mich.

126th Infantry

The 126th Infantry Regiment has been in active military service since 1855. The regiment began as militia companies in Grand Rapids. They provided the core of the Third Michigan Infantry Regiment, which served in the Civil War. After the war, the companies were reorganized as part of the Second Infantry, Michigan State Troops, the forerunner of the Michigan National Guard. When the U.S. entered World War I in 1917, the 126th was organized and assigned to the Thirty-Second "Red Arrow" Division, which was honored by the French with the Croix de Guerre for gallantry shown in the 1918 Oise-Aisne offensive. During World War II the 126th was part of the Thirty-second Division seeing action in New Guinea and the Philippines. During the war the regiment saw 654 *days of combat, more than any other American unit.The 126th Infantry Regiment has demonstrated the value of the National Guard during peacetime. Michigan National Guard units have been mobilized to assist civil authorities during strikes, riots and natural disasters. In 1873 the 126th, then the Second Regiment, quelled rioting at the Muskegon County Jail in its first peacetime role. The regiment was also mobilized during a 1909 railroad strike in Durand, the 1913 Upper Peninsula copper strike and the 1937 <u>General Motors Sit-Down Strike</u> in Flint. In July 1967 the regiment was mobilized to maintain peace during the Detroit riots. Natural disasters that required the regiment's assistance included an April 1956 tornado in the Grand Rapids area and a West Michigan blizzard in January 1878.*

Army Reserve locations in Michigan:
Ann Arbor
Battle Creek
Bay City
Fraser
Grand Rapids
Inkster
Jackson
Lansing
Livonia
Muskegon
Portage
Saginaw
Southfield
Traverse City
Waterford

Navy and Marine Corps Reserve locations in Michigan:
Navy Operations Support Center (NOSC) Battle Creek
NOSC Detroit (Selfridge ANGB)
NOSC Grand Rapids

NOSC Lansing
NOSC Saginaw

Here is the text of the Michigan state historical marker for two facilities affiliated with military operations in Michigan:

Veteran's Facility, Grand Rapids

The Michigan Veterans' Facility (formerly the Michigan Soldiers' Home) was authorized by Act 152 of the Public Acts of 1885, which provided for the establishment of a home for disabled Michigan veterans. This act resulted from the efforts of Civil War veterans who were members of the Grand Army of the Republic. The home was dedicated in December 1886 with speeches by Governor Russell A. Alger, Governor-elect Cyrus G. Luce, former Governor Austin Blair and various legislators. The need for nursing care was soon realized and in 1891 an 80-bed hospital and an 80-bed annex was added to the 320-bed main building. A 30-bed unit for women dependents was built in 1893. In 1894 the fountain and the Civil War statue in the cemetery were completed. They are the only remaining structures of that period. A new hospital was built in 1909. These buildings served Civil War veterans until 1938, when the last resident veteran of that conflict died. Veterans of the Spanish- American War and World War I were then being admitted, making construction of the Mann and Rankin buildings necessary. By 1965, World War II and Korean War veterans were using the facility in such numbers that a new concept of services was needed. This was realized in 1975, as an increasing number of Vietnam veterans required assistance, with the completion of a new building to replace many of the oldest structures. At the time of the centennial celebration in 1986, the Michigan Veterans' Facility, with the support of an employee network, veterans' organizations, the Board of Managers and volunteers continued to serve the physical, emotional and spiritual needs of many of Michigan's disabled and needy veterans.

Veteran's Hospital No. 100, Battle Creek

World War I created the need for increased medical care for returning soldiers. Veterans Hospital No. 100, a 500-bed neuropsychiatric facility that opened in 1924 on the grounds of Fort Custer, originally consisted of twenty-two Neo-Georgian structures in a crescent shaped arrangement. Like other Veterans Bureau facilities of the time, the hospital was built from standardized floor plans at a cost of nearly three million dollars. When erected on the grounds of Fort Custer, trenches, sand dunes and barren soil dominated the site. Between 1927 and 1930, 9,400 trees were planted on the 675-acre site, including English walnut trees transplanted from the Battle Creek Sanitarium that were originally grown in Mt. Vernon, Virginia.

Appendix E:
Selected Biographic Entries

While many, many people played important roles in the development of Michigan's many forts, air fields and related operations, the men listed below are highlighted because their influence extended beyond a single installation or a single battle.

Austin Blair (Library of Congress)

Blair, Austin:

Blair served as the governor of Michigan during the Civil War. Through his tireless efforts, Michigan sent some 90,000 men under arms to fight as part of the Union Army during the war. Blair made his first call to begin the formation of two regiments of volunteer infantry in January 1861–some three and a half months before the first shots of the war were fired at Fort Sumter. Blair began his political career by being elected as the Eaton County, Mich., clerk in 1842. Later, after having returned to his hometown of Jackson, Mich., he was elected to serve in the Michigan State House of Representative, 1846-1849. As a member of the state house, he introduced legislation (that ultimately failed) to allow Black citizens the right to vote. He was also a leading proponent of the successful move to abolish the death penalty in Michigan. He began his career as a member of the Whig Party, but in 1854 helped organize the Republican Party. He then served in the Michigan State Senate, 1855-1856. He was elected governor in 1860 and served in that post from 1861 to 1865. In 1864, he ran for the U.S. Senate, but lost. In 1866, he was elected to the first of three terms in the U.S. House. Camp Blair in Jackson, which operated from 1864-1866, was named in his honor. In addition, the Third Michigan Volunteer Infantry Regiment named their regimental headquarters in Washington, D.C. as Camp Blair. Blair died in 1894, age 76, in Jackson and is buried there. A statue of Michigan's "War Governor" is on the lawn of the Michigan State Capitol.

The following Michigan state historical marker about Austin Blair is posted in Jackson. A similar marker is posted in Eaton Rapids.

Austin Blair

Austin Blair began his political career in Eaton Rapids, where he was elected Eaton County clerk in 1842. As a member of the Michigan House of Representatives (1846-1849), he served in the Judiciary Committee and was a leading support-er or the 1846 law to abolish capital punishment. He also in-troduced legislation to enfranchise black citizens. He was elected Jackson County prosecutor in 1852 and served in the state senate from 1855 to 1856. Elected governor in 1860 and in 1862, Blair personally raised about $100,000 to organize *and equip the 1st Michigan Volunteer Infantry Regiment, which was the first western force to respond to Lincoln's call for troops. During the close of his active political life, Blair was a United States congressman (1867-1873) and a University of Michigan regent (1882-1890). He died in Jackson in 1894.*

Isaac Brock

Brock, Isaac

Known as the Hero of Upper Canada, Isaac Brock was a British commander who won victories at Mackinac Island and Detroit during the War of 1812. He initially joined the British Army in 1785. In 1804, as commander of the 49th Foot, he was transferred to Canada, posted in Montreal. Shortly after his arrival, Brock faced a series of soldier desertions and then a mutiny over the discipline he meted out to the captured deserters. Despite this rocky start, Brock retained his command. Anticipating the likely outbreak of hostilities in the War of 1812, Brock made preparations for war even before the official news of the declaration of war came to him. Once he did receive official notification that the U.S. and Britain were at war, Brock quickly instructed his forces to launch an attack against Mackinac Island. The U.S. garrison on the island was caught unawares and Fort Mackinac surrendered to the British. Brock then moved his army to Amherstburg, Ontario. There, Brock met the Native American warrior chief Tecumseh and the two struck up an alliance and planned an attack against Fort Detroit. For his successful capture of Detroit and Mackinac, Brock was knighted by the British crown. After his victories at Mackinac and Detroit in the summer of 1812, Brock worked diligently to shore up his defenses across Canada, in preparation of expected American counter-attacks. In October, such an attack came when New York militia cross into Ontario near Niagara Falls. Brock was at Fort George in Queenston, Ontario, about five miles from Niagara Falls when the attack came. Brock led his troops to a successful repulse of the American attack, but Brock was fatally injured during the action. He died on the night of the attack, Oct. 13, 1812. Though the British were victorious at the Battle of Queenston, the death of Brock was a devastating blow. The loss of Brock's leadership played a role in the eventual British defeat to the U.S. in the War of 1812. Several towns, schools and other institutions in Canada are named for Brock.

Hugh Brady (U.S. Army)

Brady, Hugh

Hugh Brady's father, Capt. John Brady, was killed in a battle with Native Americans during the American Revolution, while fighting on the side of the Colonial Army. Hugh Brady also served as an officer in the Continental Army, in command of a small company. Brady then served as an officer under the command of General "Mad" Anthony Wayne during the War of 1812 and was under Wayne's command during the Battle of Fallen Timbers. After the War of 1812, Brady was named commander of the U.S. 2nd Infantry Regiment. With several companies from his regiment, he re-located his command from Upstate New York to Sault Ste. Marie, and built the original Fort Brady. In 1832, Brady and his forces participated in the Black Hawk War in Illinois, primarily in a support role. In 1837, Brady was promoted to brigadier general and given command of Military Dept. No. 7, headquartered in Detroit. Brady thus provided oversight and approved of the location and construction of Fort Wilkins at Copper Harbor in 1814. Deemed too old to serve in combat in 1846 when the

Mexican-American War broke out, Brady remained in command of the forces in the Great Lakes from his posting at Detroit. In 1848, he was promoted to major general. Brady died in 1851, aged 82 and still serving as a general, after being thrown from a horse-drawn carriage in an accident while riding in Detroit.

Thornton F. Brodhead (U.S. Army)

Brodhead – Daniel; R. Thornton; and Thornton F.

Brodhead is the shared last name of at least three men who played a role in some part of Michigan's military history, Daniel; Thornton F.; and R. Thornton.

Daniel Brodhead IV (1736-1809) served with the Continental Army with distinction throughout the Revolutionary War. His first action came at the Battle of Long Island in 1776, where two notable occurrences took place: first, he was recognized by George Washington for bravery; second, his son, also named Daniel, was wounded and captured. The son would later die from the battle wounds. While in command of the 8th Pennsylvania, Brodhead was part of Gen. Lachlan McIntosh's failed March 5, 1779, attempt to capture Fort Detroit from the British. Following that failed attempt, Washington re-assigned McIntosh and gave Brodhead command of the Western Department of the Continental Army, promoting him to brigadier general in the process. Brodhead was tried at court-martial for his handling of military supplies late in the war, but was acquitted of the charges, with Washington's support. Following the war, he was one of the founders of the influential Society of the Cincinnati, a group made up primarily of Gen. George Washington's former officers. After his military service, Brodhead served in the Pennsylvania legislature and worked in state government. He appears not to be related, at least not closely, to the other two men named Brodhead, below.

Thornton Fleming Brodhead (1822-1862) was an influential figure in the middle and early part of the 19th century in Detroit. At various points he served in the state legislature, as the city's postmaster and as the editor and a part-owner of the Detroit Free Press newspaper. He was also a practicing lawyer in the city. Brodhead interrupted his professional career in the 1840s to serve as an officer with the 15th Infantry during the Mexican-American War, where he was twice honored for bravery. When the Civil War began, the Harvard-educated lawyer again donned a uniform and was appointed as the first commander of the 1st Michigan Cavalry. The unit organized at Camp Lyon, a field near the Detroit home of Brodhead, who also maintained a home on Grosse Ile. Brodhead led the 1st at the Second Battle of Manassas, also known as the Second Battle of Bull Run. After the Union cavalry had been beaten back in what was shaping up to be a major Union defeat, Brodhead tried to rally his command. He was challenged by Confederate cavalry and ordered to surrender. When Brodhead declined, he was shot in the chest by an enemy officer. He may have been the last Union casualty of that battle. He retained consciescness long enough after being shot to write a letter to his wife, in which he lambasted his senior generals for their actions at the battle, saying one had been "outwitted" and the other was a "traitor." Brodhead is the grandfather of R. Thornton Brodhead. The following Michigan historical marker is posted outside his former Grosse Ile home and office:

Colonel Brodhead's Office (20604 East River Rd., Grosse Ile)

Colonel Thornton Fleming Brodhead (1822-1862) and his wife, Archange Macomb Abbott, lived on the hill just north of this site. This small stone office and library building was constructed around 1855. Colonel Brodhead was, at various times, editor and part owner of the Detroit Free Press, state senator and postmaster at Detroit. He served in the Mexican War and led the First Michigan Cavalry in the Civil War. The colonel was mortally wounded at the Second Battle of Bull Run.

Richard Thornton Brodhead(1878-1947), grandson of Thornton F. Brodhead, would serve for more than 40 years of combined service in the Michigan Naval Militia, the Naval Reserve and the regular U.S. Navy. Brodhead, who began his career as an enlisted seaman, served on active duty with the Navy during both World War I and World War II. At the end of his career, he was a regional commander for the Naval Reserve in the Great Lakes region. Brodhead retired with the rank of captain. The Detroit Naval Armory, the construction of which he spearheaded, was named in his honor.

Cadillac, Antoine de La Mothe

Cadillac is credited as the founder of the modern city of Detroit, arriving at the site of the future city on July 24, 1701, and immediately beginning construction on Fort Ponchartrain le detroit (on the straits). Cadillac was born in France and first came to the New World in 1688, when he used the future site of Bar Harbor, Maine, for a base of exploration. After a return to France, Cadillac was appointed to take command of the Michilimackinac region and in 1695, he arrived at Fort de Buadein St. Ignace and took command of the fort. There, Cadillac was in periodic conflict with area missionaries, who accused him of selling alcohol to area Native Americans, which was forbidden by royal decree, and other questionable dealings. In 1701, Cadillac decided to re-locate his command and moved to the future site of Detroit, in an effort to better control the region's fur trade. In 1708, Cadillac was charged with a number of abuses of his authority, primarily concerning his financial dealings with area Native Americans. Cadillac was eventually cleared of the charges. In 1710, Cadillac was appointed governor of the Louisiana territory by the king of France, but he did not arrive in Louisiana until 1713, after a lengthy trip back to France. In 1716, after a series of disputes with one of the key French investors in the Louisiana territory, Cadillac was removed from the governorship. Cadillac then returned to France and lived out the remainder of his years. He died in France in 1730, age 72. Cadillac, Mich., and the Cadillac automobile brand are among many places and things that pay homage to the legacy of the French explorer.

Lewis Cass, circa 1855 (Library of Congress)

Cass, Lewis

Lewis Cass served in a wide variety of political positions, after beginning his public career as an officer in the American Army during the War of 1812. Serving under Gen. William Hull, Cass was not present at the Surrender of Detroit in 1812, but later testified against Hull in the post-war court-martial over the incident. After the war, Cass was appointed as the second governor of Michigan Territory, replacing the disgraced Hull. Cass would serve as governor for 18 years. In 1820, on one of his many trips while still governor, Cass led an expedition to map the northern Great Lakes region in an effort to find the source of the Mississippi River (the expedition got it wrong.) From 1831 to 1836, he served as Secretary of War under President Andrew Jackson. Following that, he served as U.S. Ambassador to France through 1842. In 1844, he was a candidate for president, but lost the Democratic nomination to future president James K. Polk. Cass was then elected to the U.S. Senate from Michigan, but only served half of his six-year term. He resigned to run for president as the Democratic nominee in 1848, losing to Zachary Taylor. He was re-elected to the U.S. Senate from Michigan and served about eight years. He was then named as the Secretary of State under James Buchanan, 1857-1860. Cass died in 1866 and is among many local luminaries buried in Detroit's Elmwood Cemetery.

Woodcut image of La Salle's ship, Le Griffon.

De La Salle, Sieur (aka Rene-Robert Cavelier and Robert de La Salle)

Trained as a Jesuit priest, though he never took his final vows, Rene-Robert Cavelier was born in France in 1643. Sieur de La Salle opened the Great Lakes and the Mississippi River region to European traders. His explorations and exploits set in motion a chain of events that eventually saw European settlers oust numerous Native American tribes from their homelands, prompting years of conflict and ending in the creation of the United States. "Sieur" translates from French as "sir." Le Salle departed France for what was then called "New France"–encompassing huge portions of Canada and the central U.S.--in 1666. Le Salle was ever interested in expanding the trading empire of New France and made numerous trips of exploration around the Great Lakes and down the Mississippi River. Upon reaching the mouth of the Mississippi River on April 9, 1682, Le Salle declared that the entire Mississippi River basin to be named Louisiana in honor of French King Louis XIV. In 1679, he and an expedition set out in a 45-ton barque called Le Griffon, and sailed from their outpost in Ontario through Lakes Erie and Huron, reaching Michilimackinac. They then sailed on to Green Bay, Wisconsin. There, La Salle and a group left Le Griffon and traveled south down the western shore of Lake Michigan, rounded the southern end of the lake and ended in current St. Joseph, Mich., where they built Fort Miami in late 1679. Le Salle's party left Fort Miami shortly thereafter, destroying Fort Miami as they departed. They spent the next several years in exploration on the Mississippi River and elsewhere. In 1682, Le Salle returned to France to seek supplies and colonists for a planned new settlement on the Gulf of Mexico. Many of his men in that mission were lost in a series of problems and his remaining men mutinied, leading to La Salle's death March 19, 1687, in modern-day Texas. Numerous locations in the U.S. are named in honor of La Salle or have other legacies to the French explorer. After Le Salle left the ship Le Griffon, the ship was never heard from again. In 2004–325 years after Le Griffon was lost--the ship's possible remains were discovered in northwest Lake Michigan, prompting a dispute between the state of Michigan, the nation of France and the diver who discovered the remains over the rights to the remains. The three parties eventually agreed to co-operate in the exploration of the remains. A major dive on the remains began in the summer of 2013. An image of La Salle is on page 105.

Charles Gratiot. (U.S. Army)

Gratiot, Charles

A member of the fourth graduating class at West Point, Charles Gratiot worked as an engineer under the command of Alexander Macomb in his first assignment in the Army. During the War of 1812, he built Fort Meigs in Perrysberg, Ohio, and was then sent to the Port Huron, Mich., area, where he constructed what became known as Fort Gratiot on the 128-year-old remains of Fort St. Joseph. Gratiot later was part of the U.S. force that failed to capture Mackinac Island in the summer of 1814. Following the U.S. victory in the War of 1812, he received a proclamation of "Thanks of Congress" for his actions during the war. He was the Army's chief of engineers for the Michigan territory for two years after the war and was then assigned as the superintendent of the military works at Hampton Roads, Virg. In 1828, Gratiot was promoted to general and named chief engineer for the entire Army, a position he held for 10 years. He was dismissed from his duties in 1838 in a dispute over his handling of government funds. Despite that dispute, he was able to land a job as a clerk in the government land office in St. Louis, Mo., and stayed in that post for 15 years. He died in St. Louis in 1855 at age 68.

William Hull, painting by Rembrandt Peale

Hull, William

William Hull will forever be known as the general who surrendered Detroit to the British in the War of 1812, an offense for which he was sentenced to be executed. A native of Connecticut, Hull was a young lawyer in his home state when the American Revolution touched off. He served as an officer in the war, serving in a number of major campaigns and was later recognized by both George Washington and the Continental Congress for his service. Before the war, Hull was a close friend of Nathan Hale and Hull was primarily responsible for publicizing Hale's famed last words: "I only regret that I have but one life to lose for my country." Following the war, Hull served as a judge and state senator in Massachusetts. In 1805, President Thomas Jefferson appointed Hull to be the first governor of the newly-created Michigan

Territory. Two years later, Hull negotiated the Treaty of Detroit with a number of area Native American tribes, gaining most of southeast Michigan for the new U.S.A. When the War of 1812 broke out, Hull, who was 60 years old, initially resisted efforts to appoint himself as a General of the Army of the Northwest, though he eventually accepted the commission. Hull endured a number of setbacks, mostly attributable to poor communications–he didn't find out war had been declared until well after most of the unfriendly forces around in him were already taking action against him–and poor advance planning by the young federal government. Encamped as the senior officer at Fort Detroit in August 1812–and still serving as governor of Michigan Territory, Hull faced a far better organized British force. Harassed as well by Native American warriors, Hull surrendered Fort Detroit to British forces led by Sir Isaac Brock on Aug. 16, 1812. Two other politicians in Hull's command, then-Col. Lewis Cass and Lt. Col. Robert Lucas, testified that the surrender was entirely the fault of Hull and Hull was sentenced to be shot by court-martial judge Gen. Henry Dearborn, later the Secretary of War and namesake of the suburban Detroit city. Cass was soon appointed as the next governor of Michigan and Lucas became governor of Ohio. Hull was later pardoned by President James Madison. Hull spent the remainder of his life living in Massachusetts and wrote two books in an effort to clear his name. He died in 1825. Though he was the first governor of Michigan Territory, his name has largely disappeared from the state, except in history books.

Marquette, Father Jacques:

The name of French-born Jesuit priest Pere (Father) Jacques Marquette looms large over Michigan's Upper Peninsula. Marquette was the founder of the European settlements in Sault Ste. Marie and in St. Ignace, as well as Ashland, Wisconsin. He founded his mission in Sault Ste. Marie in 1668–making the Soo the first city in Michigan--and in St. Ignace in 1671. Some suggest that the mission at St. Ignace may have had a stockade around it at some point. If so, it was the first "fort" in Michigan. In 1673, Marquette joined an expedition with fellow Frenchmen Louis Jolliet. The Jolliet-Marquette Expedition became the first Europeans to explore the Upper Mississippi River basin. They made it to within about 400 miles of the Gulf of Mexico before turning back. In 1675, as he was making his way back to the mission in St. Ignace, Marquette was struck ill from dysentery, which he had contracted on the expedition. He died at age 37 near the present-day city of Ludington, Mich. Two years later, his remains were moved and re-buried at the mission in St. Ignace. The Upper Peninsula city of Marquette, Mich., is one of many, many locations named in honor of the priest.

The following Michigan state historical marker is located in Frankfort, Mich., near the site of Marquette's death:

Marquette's Death

On May 18, 1675, Father Jacques Marquette, the great Jesuit missionary and explorer, died and was buried by two French companions somewhere along the Lake Michigan shore of the lower peninsula. Marquette had been returning to his mission at St. Ignace which he had left in 1873 to go on an exploring trip to the Mississippi and the Illinois country. The exact location of Marquette's death has long been a subject of controversy. Evidence presented in the 1960's indicates that this site, near the natural outlet of the Betsie River, at the northeast corner of a hill which was here until 1900, is the Marquette death site and that the Betsie is the Riviere du Pere Marquette of early French accounts and maps. Marquette's bones were reburied at St. Ignace in 1677.

Pontiac, Chief

Namesake of cities both in Michigan and Illinois, Chief Pontiac of the Ottawa tribe also gave his name to a series of battles and military campaigns in which various Native American tribes pushed back against an ever-expanding presence of European settlers in the Great Lakes region. Together, these battles in 1763-1766 came to be known as Pontiac's Rebellion. Pontiac is believed to have fought on the side of the French during the French & Indian War, 1754-1763. British victory in that war led to even further animosity between the British and many of the Native American tribes around the Great Lakes. On April 27, 1763, Pontiac spoke at a council meeting of various tribal leaders in what is now Council Point Park in Lincoln Park, Mich. There, he encouraged attacks on various British interests in the region. Most notably, Pontiac and about 300 warriors launched a surprise attack on Fort Detroit on May 9, 1763. British commander Henry Gladwin got word of Pontiac's planned surprise and Pontiac began a siege of the fort. Over the summer, Pontiac's forces devastated a British supply mission to the fort that arrived unaware of the siege and held off a rescue force of some 250 British regulars sent to the fort in what became known as the Battle of Bloody Run. On Oct. 31, 1763, tired of waiting for the French to come to his aid for a final attack on Fort Detroit, Pontiac withdrew the siege and moved into Ohio. Eventually he negotiated a peace with the British. In 1768, Pontiac moved into Illinois. On April 20, 1769, under conditions that remain somewhat murky, Pontiac was murdered by a member of the Peoria tribe in the village of Cahokia, Ill. His final burial place is uncertain. Historians differ on the impact Pontiac had on the wider rebellion that bore his name. Some say he was merely a local leader, others suggest he was instrumental in orchestrating actions against the British across the Great Lakes region.

Sinclair, Patrick

A native of Scotland, Sinclair enlisted in the British Army around 1754 and served briefly in the Caribbean. Serving with the 42nd Foot, his unit was sent to upstate New York and there embarked on a move against French forces in Montreal, Quebec. During that campaign, Sinclair was given command of a French ship on the St. Lawrence River. He then transferred to the Royal Marines and held command of several ships on Lake Ontario. Acting in response to Pontiac's Rebellion of 1763, Sinclair became the first known European to lead a ship-board expedition into the Upper Great Lakes in almost a century. In 1764, he oversaw the construction of Fort St. Clair in the modern-day town of St. Clair, not far from Port Huron. He stayed there only briefly, continuing his command mostly at sea on Lakes Erie, Huron and Superior for the next three years. In 1767, British forces were reduced in the region and Sinclair lived for two years at the fort that bore his name. In 1769, he returned to England, though actively sought a posting in Michigan or Canada. Finally, in 1775, he was appointed superintendent and lieutenant governor of Michilimackinac (modern Mackinaw City). Due largely to the U.S. Revolution, Sinclair did not reach Fort Michilimackinac until 1779. Shortly after arrival, he scouted out a new location for his fort and headquarters–on Mackinac Island. On May 12, 1781, he purchased the island from the local Ojibwa tribe for 5,000 pounds. In 1780, he led a force, made up of a few British regulars and about 1,000 Native American warriors, to Wisconsin, down into Illinois and then down the Mississippi River to attack Spanish forces in and around St. Louis, Mo. The Spanish repulsed his attacks and Sinclair returned to Mackinac Island. In 1782, questions arose about his spending patterns and management of military funds. For two years, he lived in Quebec, fighting to clear his name. In 1784, he returned to Scotland and, still fighting questions over his handling of government funds, was briefly thrown into London's Newgate prison for debt accrued by paying his legal bills. Eventually his name was cleared, but he was in financial ruins. He remained on half-pay at his home in Scotland, never able to fully clear his debts. He died in 1820. His final rank was lieutenant general. Lake St. Clair and St. Clair County both carry on his name.

Anthony Wayne

Wayne, Anthony:

Now remembered more for his nickname – "Mad" Anthony Wayne – than his military exploits, Wayne served as a general in the Continental Army during the Revolutionary War. In legacy to his service, numerous cities, counties, schools and other entities are named for Wayne in more than a dozen states. Wayne's nickname came from what is almost universally described as his "fiery" disposition. It was Gen. Wayne's army that took possession of Fort Detroit on July 11, 1796, placing Detroit under an American flag for the first time. Wayne himself, however, was not in Detroit on that day, but would arrive several weeks later. Though he served with great distinction at many battles throughout the Revolutionary War, Wayne's actions after the war may have been his most significant. Several years after the war ended, Wayne was recalled to military service personally by President George Washington and given command of the "Legion of the United States." With the Legion, Wayne was involved in a series of battles between the new U.S. and British-backed Native American tribes along what was then the new nation's northwest border. Over a two-year period, Wayne's army built a string of forts, primarily in Pennsylvania, Ohio and Indiana, to garrison the frontier. The most significant conflict during that period took place in August 1794 in the Battle of Fallen Timbers, which took place around modern-day Toledo, Ohio. In that battle, Wayne's forces recorded an overwhelming victory against British forces and a coalition of Native American tribes aligned with the British. The presence of the new forts, coupled with his victory at Fallen Timbers, moved much of the Lower Great Lakes region into control of the new United States, paving the way for the departure of the British forces at Fort Detroit. On Aug. 3, 1795, Wayne negotiated the Treaty of Greenville with several Native American tribes. In exchange for about $20,000 worth of goods, the Native Americans ceded an area of land that stretches from Toledo to Detroit to Chicago. Article 3, Item 12 of the treaty states, *"The post of Detroit, and all the land to the north, the west and the south of it, of which the Indian title has been extinguished by gifts or grants to the French or English governments: and so much more land to be annexed to the district of Detroit, as shall be comprehended between the river Rosine, on the south, lake St. Clair on the north, and a line, the general course whereof shall be six miles distant from the west end of lake*

Erie and Detroit river. "Less than 10 years after the Battle at Fallen Timbers, Ohio became the 17th state in the Union, with Indiana and Michigan eventually to follow. While still serving as a major general and just months after he took possession of Detroit, Wayne died Dec. 15, 1796, age 51, while en route home to Pennsylvania from Fort Detroit, from complications from gout. Wayne's death came less than 2 ½ years after his victory at Fallen Timbers. In between his periods of military service, Wayne served briefly in the state legislature in his home state of Pennsylvania and then as a member of the Second U.S. Congress, though he served less than a full, single term due to a dispute over his residency status. During Wayne's military service in the 1790s, he was the senior officer in the Army, a forerunner to the positions of Commanding General of the Army and today's chief of staff of the Army position.

Appendix F:

10 Most Significant Events in Michigan's Military History
(Presented in chronological order)

Founding of Fort Miami by Sieur de La Salle, November 1679 - - This fort, in modern-day St. Joseph, Mich., was the first true military fort created in the state of Michigan. De La Salle is the famed explorer of the Mississippi River and launched his 1681 mission to the Mississippi River from Fort Miami. De Le Salle was a Frenchman and the fort was an outpost of the Kingdom of France. The fort was destroyed by De La Salle's men as they departed in 1681.

Founding of Fort Pontchartrain, July 24, 1701 -- Antoine de la Mothe Cadillac arrived on Grosse Ile on July 23, 1701. The following day, he arrived on the mainland in what is now down-town Detroit. Construction began immediately on Fort Pontchar-train, named for the French official who authorized Cadillac to leave Fort de Buade in St. Ignace, and move to location on the lower Great Lakes. From Detroit, Cadillac claimed the surrounding territory in the name of France and sought to control the surround-ing fur trade. The first completed building in the new settlement was the original Ste. Anne's Church, which was the first estab-lished European church in southeast Michigan and is believed to be the second oldest Catholic parish in continual operation in the U.S. The walls of the stockade, made of logs and measuring some 12 feet high in the corner battlements, were completed shortly thereafter. The fort was controlled by France through 1760; by Britain, 1760-1795; and the U.S., from 1795 until it was destroyed in the Great Detroit Fire on June 11, 1805. The fort had been replaced by Fort Lernoult in 1778 (later called Fort Shelby), but remnants of the original fort were used for various purposes until the 1805 fire.

The Lacrosse Game at Fort Michilimackinac, June 2, 1763 -- In the spring of 1763, the Native American uprising known as Pontiac's Rebellion challenged British forts around the Great Lakes region. Despite these high tensions, British commanders at Fort Michilimackinac in Mackinaw City (located today at the foot of the Mackinac Bridge) planned a big celebration on June 2, 1763, in honor of King George III's birthday. As part of the celebration, local Chippewas arranged a game of baggatiway–a forerunner of the modern game of lacrosse–with a visiting group of warriors from the Sac tribe. The game was played right outside the gates of the fort and the British soldiers came out to watch and join in the festive mood. During the game, the ball was "accidentally" thrown over the fort walls and some players ran inside the fort to retrieve it. This was the pre-arranged signal for the Chippewas and Sacs to attack the soldiers. About half of the garrison's soldiers were killed in the attack and the remainder captured. The Native Americans then left the fort, but the British presence in the Straits of Mackinac area was significantly curtailed for about a year. A re-enactment of the game is staged annually outside of the re-created Fort Michilimackinac, which is now operated as a state park.

Surrender of Detroit, Aug. 15-16, 1812 – Also known as the Siege of Detroit and the Battle of Fort Detroit. As part of the War of 1812, a British force of about 330 regulars, under the command of Major General Isaac Brock, reinforced with about twice as many Native American warriors, led by the Shawnee leader Tecumseh, and some 400 Canadian militia prepared to attack Fort Detroit, with 582 regulars and more than 1,600 militia under the command of American Brigadier Gen. William Hull. In early August 1812, Brock set up an artillery battery in Windsor, Ontario, across the Detroit River from Fort Detroit. On Aug. 15, Brock sent Hull an ultimatum, demanding the Americans' surrender. Hull refused. The next morning, supported by his artillery and the cannons of two British ships in the river, Brock crossed into Detroit and began to march on the fort. Fearing a massacre at the hands of Brock's Native American allies–a threat made in Brock's second ultimatum–Hull surrendered the fort. Hull would later be court-martialed and sentenced to be shot for his surrender, but was eventually pardoned by President James Madison. The British Army controlled the fort for about a year until suffering reverses in the region as a result of a defeat in the Battle of Lake Erie. With British naval forces scattered, a U.S. force of about 1,000 soldiers, under the command of future president William Henry Harrison, marched on the fort, prompting the British to leave the fort and retreat back into Canada. The U.S. forces entered the fort on Sept. 29, 1813, and shortly thereafter named it Fort Shelby. Detroit has been an American city ever since.

Battle of Mackinac Island, July 26-Aug. 4, 1814 – On July 18, 1812, a force of British regulars and Native Americans captured Fort Mackinac and Mackinac Island in an event known as the Siege of Fort Mackinac. The British attack came in the early days of the War of 1812, apparently before the U.S. forces in the fort were aware that war had been declared. As a result, the unprepared Americans quickly surrendered. The British spent the next year strengthening their hold on the strategic island, including building another fort, Fort George, on the island's highest point. Finally, on July 26, 1814, after several delays, which provided ample warning for the British that the Americans were on their way–a force of 700 American soldiers made their way to the island. Following two days of ineffectual naval bombardment, the Americans landed on the island. Despite their overwhelming numbers–the British force counted only 140 regulars and about as many Native American allies–the Americans were quickly repulsed. The U.S. suffered more than a dozen casualties, including one of their commanders, Major Andrew Holmes. The war ended in December 1814 with an American victory and in July 1815, the U.S. reoccupied the island and Fort Mackinac. Fort George was renamed Fort Holmes in honor of the fallen commander of the failed attack. Fort Mackinac closed as a military installation in 1895 and has been a beloved tourist attraction ever since.

Battle of Toledo, 1835-1836 -- Also known as the Toledo War or the Michigan-Ohio War, this "war" was more of a legislative dispute between the state of Ohio and the territory of Michigan. Due to some (possibly intentional) legislative misreading of maps of the times – or possibly due to inaccuracies in the maps themselves – both Ohio and Michigan laid claim to a roughly 468-square mile strip of land, known as the Toledo Strip. The issue came to a head when Michigan applied for statehood in 1835 and included the Toledo Strip in its official request. Both Ohio, under Gov. Robert Lucas–namesake of today's Lucas County which includes modern Toledo–and Michigan, under Gov. Stevens T. Mason – known as the "boy governor" -- called up militia forces to do battle over the strip, but these militias essentially existed to allow each side to engage in exaggerated name calling and related gamesmanship. The two forces did meet once, but no shots were fired. On July 15, 1835, Monroe, Mich., deputy sheriff Joseph Wood went into Toledo to arrest Ohio Militia Major Benjamin Stickney. In the scuffle that followed, Wood was stabbed by one of Stickney's sons–the only injury of the "war." Wood survived his wounds. In the summer of 1836, Congress suggested a compromise–Michigan would get the Upper Peninsula in exchange for giving up claims to Toledo. The measure was voted on and rejected by a Michigan territorial convention held in September. Toledo was seen as the real prize–the U.P. was primarily wilderness held by Native American tribes at the time. Later in 1836, Congress and President Andrew Jackson further pressured Michigan to accept the deal, holding up the question of Michigan statehood until the deal was accepted. Finally, at another convention on Dec. 14, 1836–known the "Frozen Convention" for the bitter cold that year–Michigan accepted the deal. About a month later, Michigan was accepted into the union as a state. A couple of years later, copper and iron were discovered in the U.P. and the perceived value of the U.P. skyrocketed.

"Thank God for Michigan," May 16, 1861 – It cannot be definitively confirmed that President Abraham Lincoln did in fact utter those words during the Civil War, but enough sources report on them that they have taken on the air of both fact and legend. In his annual January address to the State Legislature, Michigan Gov. Austin Blair pledged to raise two militia regiments to support the Union cause–more than three months before shots were first fired at Fort Sumter, South Carolina, April 12, 1861. After that battle at Fort Sumter, when a desperate federal government called upon the states to send militia to defend the Union, Michigan was ready to respond. As Michigan's 1st Volunteer Regiment marched into Washington, the beleaguered Lincoln is said to have exclaimed "Thank God for Michigan!" Michigan units went on to serve with distinction throughout the war, including a key cavalry unit serving under Gen. George Armstrong Custer at Gettysburg and another Michigan unit that captured former Confederate President Jefferson Davis after the surrender of Confederate forces.

Opening of Selfridge Field, July 1, 1917 -- One of the original military air fields in the nation, Selfridge has contributed American Airmen to every one of the nation's conflicts since World War I. During World War II, a unit of the all-Black "Tuskegee Airmen" were assigned to the base for training. After the terror attacks of Sept. 11, 2001, fighter aircraft from Selfridge patrolled the skies over the Detroit region for several years. Today, Selfridge Air National Guard Base is home to units of the Air Force, Army, Navy, Marine Corps, Coast Guard and Border Patrol.

Arsenal of Democracy, 1941-1945 – During World War II, approximately 25,000 tanks and almost 8,700 B-24 bombers were built at industrial plants in Warren and Ypsilanti, respectively. Across the Detroit region, some 350,000 workers contributed directly to the war effort, building everything from Jeeps to machine gun parts, and patrol boats to civil defense radios. The production of the region prompted U.S. President Franklin Roosevelt to declare Detroit "the great Arsenal of Democracy." Today, southeast Michigan continues to be a key national hub of military production and procurement, largely centered around the Detroit Arsenal in Warren, which was initially responsible for all those tanks in World War II.

Air Force Drawdown, 1970s-present – During the early days of the Cold War, Michigan was home to four major Air Force bases, each of which at one time supported the mission of the Air Force's storied Strategic Air Command–charged with the nuclear deterrent mission during those tense years of stand-off with the Soviet Union. Over the years, first Kincheloe AFB, then Wurtsmith AFB, then K.I. Sawyer AFB, near Sault Ste. Marie, Oscoda and Marquette, respectively, were closed. In 1971, Selfridge AFB was transferred from the active duty Air Force to the Michigan Air National Guard and over the years the level of activity at Selfridge has been greatly curtailed.

Made in the USA
Charleston, SC
29 March 2014